Little Miss Less-Than-Perfect

Why women dabble in the art of comparison

Karen Mutchler Allen

Guest Author

Michele Fort

This book is dedicated to Lindsey. Thank you for believing in me. I love you more than you know. This is also dedicated to my amazing sister, Veronica. I love you.

Table of Contents

Foreword

As Karen so eloquently unveils in "Little Miss Less-Than-Perfect"...COMPARISON is an ultimate confidence crushing, joy killing, peace THIEF. It's a stronghold that all humans wrestle with from time to time, but for women in particular...it's a brutal adversary. Although ego plays its role in many aspects of comparison...for most of us it's not as much about the drive to succeed in society as it is about our own emotional assurance. For women this internal conflict isn't primarily focused on another's list of accomplishments, but rather on finding our own personal space, place, and "significance" in the world and mostly-the great fear we have of losing it. I'll cut straight to the chase and share a main reason that I believe we feel the reoccurring prick and puncture of this proverbial "thorn" in our flesh. Anytime someone's personal significance is threatened in the presence of another, sadly we can become "secret haters" *metaphorically and often times literally* of the "little-miss- perfect-ones" whose incredibleness makes us feel inadequate and insignificant. With women it's not always about prestige or the magnitude of another woman's strong suit...it's more about the burning intensity and rise of insecurity that floods over us when someone has a natural, effortless ability to do a common, everyday thing that we're struggling, scraping and screaming just to maintain. It doesn't have to be a monumental thing at all—it can be a mundane area of life that someone else has "together" that just so happens to be falling apart on us. I was a first time mother at 18, a stay-at- home mom by nature, purpose, and personal preference. In the early 80's-- my type was a rare oddity and being a stay-at- home mom wasn't as celebrated as it is today. In that era, if you didn't have a "real" job outside of the home, many thought of you as being lazy, unproductive, and not contributing anything worthwhile to the family.

I had no mother present in my life as a child, so I willfully sacrificed personal luxuries and conveniences so that I could be at home fulltime with my babies. I rarely ever spent a dime for anything that wasn't an absolute necessity. My heart was content as it could be living in my lil' doublewide and taking care of my family. However, it seemed to annoy other women that I could easily live without luxuries that they couldn't live without. They were resentful and insulting because I didn't base my identity on the things that they based theirs on. I just felt blessed that God allowed me the opportunity to sit in the middle of my sea-foam green "trailer" carpet and love on my babies every day. They couldn't believe this life was ultimately satisfying for me, but it really was. They didn't believe it because they were imagining themselves having to live in my world...knowing their personality and perception of success was much different than mine. I admired these successful women and their positions in society, but eventually the critical spirits who looked and spoke down to me, finally got the best of me. Their words devalued me into feeling like a complete failure for simply being who I was. At least two or three times a year I would lose focus, second guess myself...and wish that I could be like them. I felt insecure and disappointed that God didn't design me to naturally be a career woman like them, instead of the nurturing mother "ME" that He created me to be. Those who were critical "admittedly" admired me from a distance and were secretly envious of certain qualities I had that didn't come easy for them. This is how subtlety the "seeds of comparison" are sown and become rooted...and how they viciously strip beautiful souls of their confidence.

The truth is, being a stay-at- home mom is a very legit and vital role to play in the lives of our children and ultimately in society...but so is being a successful business owner, a compassionate nurse, a dedicated teacher, a top-notched attorney or the president of a corporation. No certain path is any more or less significant than the next, as each one fulfills a unique purpose. We are all essential in our being and in the kingdom of God. He has given us both natural and spiritual gifts as He purposed in his heart was best. Although some have a more obvious leadership role that requires being seen and heard more...the behind-the- scenes servant roles are no less significant or impressive. Both are equally necessary to make the world go around. As women we were never meant to compete or compare ourselves with one another. We were sent to walk out our earth journey with a unique mission to complete while we're here. When we scheme, sabotage, envy, critically judge others and ourselves, resent and compare our weakness to another's strength...we are smothering out essential flames in the bright and eternal LIGHT of the world that He destined us to keep ablaze. As important as it is for us to find our personal significance and place, we have a desperate need for each other's love, impartation, support and encouragement...in accomplishing all that we were sent forth to accomplish. We aren't enemies...nor are we competitors. We're women-- and we are one and the same. When one of us wins, we are ALL winning.

Our significance isn't in our appearance-- or in the size of our jeans. Neither is it in our financial successes or the lack thereof. It isn't found in what we have been able to accomplish for ourselves, or in the various ways we are gifted. However wonderful-- our significance isn't based on any of these aspects--it is based entirely on WHOSE we are. We are significant only because of the GREATNESS that we are connected to. When we compliment and celebrate each other's strengths and cover each other's weaknesses instead of preying upon them--we are empowering each other to stand bravely in our righteous, rightful position in this united coalition that God assembled us to be.

It is my honor and privilege to introduce this powerful book, "Little Miss-Less- Than-Perfect". It's a humorous, serious, plentiful reservoir filled with transparency and priceless nuggets of wisdom that will bring enlightenment, understanding, and wholeness to every woman's heart. Karen digs deep down below the surface of the superficial and into the psyche of our soul-- to shed light on this darkness that prevents us from being the best version of ourselves that we could possibly be. In her book she exposes and confronts the elephant in the room. The huge one that continually stomps our spirit-- the one that has hindered and sapped our emotional energy and spiritual expansion for long enough! May the revelation you glean from this reading experience birth a revolution in your life!

~Denise Smith
Author of Seeds of Purpose

"This is what the Sovereign Lord says: Come from the four winds, O breath, and breathe into these slain, that they may live. So I prophesied as he commanded me, and breath entered them; they came to life and stood up on their feet
--a vast army."
Ezekiel 37:9-10

You, beloved, are the army...

Acknowledgments

To Brittany Cash: Thank you so much for using your amazing artistic talent for the cover. You are wonderfully gifted! Thank you!

To Denise Smith, a fellow author and someone whom I look up to immensely: Thank you for taking the time and energy to write the foreword to this book. I'm so grateful for the gift of your words but even more grateful for the gift of your belief in me. Thank you.

To Michele Fort, my word-girl: I really cannot thank you enough for being my guest author. I can't think of anyone else I'd rather share a book with than you. You are a gifted writer, talented far beyond your understanding. He will continue to use your words to impact the multitudes. He told me so. I love you, my precious friend.

To Teresa Bishop, Terri Torbett, Mary Hanson, Sarah Register, Crista Andrews, Trish Pearce, Kathy Mutchler, Veronica Sanders, Rhonda Stamey, and Kelly Barfield: Thank you for saying yes! The prayers that you have written and prayed over all these amazing women who will read this book will forever bless my soul. "The prayer of a righteous man (or in this case, woman) is powerful and effective." James 5:16 Thank you all so, so, much!

To Marian Wharton: Thank you for using your gifts as an English Teacher on my book! You took on the feat of proof-reading over 40,000 words and did an amazing job! Thank you so very much friend!

To Lindsey, Ryleigh, Josey, and Garrison Allen: Thank you doesn't even begin to cover it. Thank you for letting me write, and write, and write. In doing so, you are letting me be who God created me to be and for that, I'm eternally grateful.

Introduction

Ya'll...there she is. You know, "her". Little Miss Perfect. She's standing in the local coffee shop as I sit in the corner booth. She's perfect. Like, seriously perfect. Her hair is long, beautiful, and completely the opposite color of mine and for some reason, it seems to be blowing in the wind like a shampoo commercial...except we are in the middle of a coffee shop. Weird. Anyway, there she stands, like a goddess. The Coffee Shop Goddess. And ya'll...she's wearing white pants...white pants...and she looks amazing in them. What? Is that even possible? To look GOOD in white pants? The only muffin top she has is sitting in her perfectly manicured hand...and it's an organic blueberry one. Her other graceful hand gently grips a tall Green Tea Chai Latte. I see her smile at the cashier...and of course, her smile is, well, you know...perfect. I bet she was born with teeth like that and didn't even need braces. Stupid straight, white teeth. I almost didn't want to look at her anymore but I couldn't help myself. It's like looking at a car accident on the highway. You don't want to look but you don't want to NOT look either. My eyes focus in on her face. As I do, I hear angels singing. Real angels were actually singing because her face was like one of their own. Flawless. Wrinkle and bump free, just like her white pants. Apparently, at that very moment, she could feel someone staring at her angelic face and her breathtaking, ocean blue eyes lock with mine. I half smile, half grimace, then quickly avert my eyes. Little Miss Perfect turns to leave the coffee shop and exits as the little bell on the door rings, as if to say, "I'll miss you...you are perfect." I've always hated that stupid bell. I watch her leave through the window. And that's when it happens. I catch a glimpse of myself in that window. I see what she saw...and it isn't good...like...at all. My hair is wadded up in a "mom-bun" on the top of my head. Not the cute, hip kind of bun but the "I haven't washed my hair in....wait what day is it?" kind of bun. I see the laugh lines around my eyes that used to only be there when I laughed, now they just stay there, like they are laughing at me. I stare at my hands. They look old. They look tired. They look like my grandma's. There is no manicure to be found on these nails, at least not one in the past three months. Some nails are broken. Some nails still have a little of the pewter grey polish on them. Some don't. I shrug a sad shrug and sigh. Then I look at my pants. I'm not sure you can call sweat pants real pants but that's what I am wearing. And, to add insult to my sweat pant-wearing injury, there is also a huge stain on the thigh. Like ginormous. I don't even know exactly WHAT the stain is. I'd love to tell you that I didn't know it was there when I put them on this morning, but that would be a lie. I saw it. I saw it and wore them anyway.

So I sit here, at this corner booth, with my white chocolate mocha and my cinnamon bun...and a very large muffin top (not the organic kind, the kind that needs a sit-up and a salad). My mind, my heart, my soul all feel crushed. Broken. Smashed. Small. Empty. Little Miss Less-Than-Perfect. That is me. That is my name. That is who I am. The comparison game begins. But this is a game no one ever wins. Ever.

All the Fat...

Have you ever wondered where it all started? Where did this, "I'm going to compare myself to you and see how good or bad I feel about myself" mentality begin? Well, it started in the beginning. Yup, like in the beginning beginning.

Adam and Eve (see...I told you it was in the beginning!) had two sons, Cain and Abel. Their third son, Seth, came a little later. Cain was the first born and worked the fields. From what we know, he was a great gardener and tended to the fruits and vegetables of the land. Abel was the second born son and he was in charge of the flock or the livestock.

It came time for an offering to be made to the Lord. Let's pick up the story in Genesis 4:3-5. "In the course of time Cain brought some of the fruits of the soil as an offering to the LORD. But Abel brought fat portions from some of the firstborn of his flock. The LORD looked with favor on Abel and his offering, but on Cain and his offering he did not look with favor. So Cain was very angry, and his face was downcast."

So, basically what happened was both brothers brought a sacrifice to the Lord, Cain his fruits and Abel his meats. I can see in my head how this may have gone down. Cain drags his big basket of fruit to the altar. Heaves it up onto the rocks. Steps back and thinks to himself, "Now THAT is a big basket of fruit. It's not all my best fruit, I saved some of those for dinner later, but it's mostly the good stuff. I sure am good at this gardening thing!" Then, his little brother shows up. He brings a sled full of animal fat from the firstborn of the flock he tends. Abel asks Cain to help him hoist the sled full of animal fat on top of the altar beside Cain's altar. It takes the both of them to lift the sacrifice onto the altar. They are both panting and sweating as they finally step back and look at the two altars. All of a sudden, in Cain's eyes, they were no longer altars but weighted scales. And his scale was light. He sees the fat of his brother's offering and is reminded of what God demands in a sacrifice. Leviticus 3:16 says, "The priest shall burn them on the altar as food, an offering made by fire, a pleasing aroma. All the fat is the LORD'S." First off, can I just say that I wish all my fat was the Lord's. It's not. It belongs to Chic Fil A's milkshakes. And McDonald's fries. And Wendy's burgers. And a lot of it belongs to Krispy Kreme. So, yeah, definitely not the Lord's fat.

Anyway, the Lord then declared that He was pleased with Abel's sacrifice but was not pleased with Cain's. Why did God not accept Cain's offering? The reason wasn't because God was a carnivore instead of a vegetarian. It was because God saw the heart behind each offering. He can do that you know, He can see our hearts...through the fruit and through the meat...He can see the motive, the attitude, the purpose...and He knows what is worthy of Him and what is not. So now we are left with a very angry Cain. Why? Why was he so mad?

Cain was mad because he had played the comparison game and realized he didn't measure up. His offering wasn't good enough. He wasn't good enough. In that moment he compared himself to who he was and who he wasn't in regards to his brother and he didn't like the outcome. See, the farmer had compared himself to the shepherd. Instead of searching his OWN heart to see what would be acceptable to God and let God show him what his best would be, he measured it against Abel's. Cain could have looked at his own basket of fruit and come to the conclusion that God would not be pleased with his lack of a thoughtful and sacrificial offering. Instead, he lined up both offerings, compared the content, and was angry with the result. So, Cain measured the offerings and knew he had come up short. Then, the Lord called him out on it. Not for the comparison, but for the disrespect and apathy of the offering and the heart behind it. Genesis 4:6-7 "Then the LORD said to Cain, "Why are you angry? Why is your face downcast? If you do what is right, will you not be accepted? But if you do not do what is right sin is crouching at your door; it desires to have you, but you must master it." He had played the comparison game...and he had lost. But Cain wasn't the only loser.

The rest of the story doesn't go well for Abel. Yes, Abel. Genesis 4:8 "Now Cain said to his brother Abel, "Let's go out to the field." And while they were in the field, Cain attacked his brother and killed him." So Cain gets his brother alone and kills him. He killed his own brother. Sibling rivalry at its worst. Now, I must admit, I've kicked my brother in the "boy-parts" before when I was mad at him but I've never tried to kill him. He did stay down on the ground for a while though. I do feel kind of bad about that now. Well, sort of.

Cain's battle with comparison ended with loss. Lots of it. Adam and Eve lost a son. Two in fact. God tells Cain that he is cursed and that he will wander the earth. He is estranged, a nomad, wandering in the land of Nod. It also says in Genesis 4:16 that Cain went out from the LORD's presence. That meant Cain no longer was able to dwell with the Lord, talk with Him or be with Him. When it came to the Lord, Cain was hidden. The absence of the Lord's presence was another consequence

> Comparison is a thief. It steals. It kills. It destroys.

of Cain's choices. He didn't lose the opportunity to be in God's presence because he compared his offering to his brothers. He lost that opportunity because he acted on the feelings that comparison brings. What a high price to pay. Adam and Eve lost both of their sons because of this dangerous comparison game. You'll hear this phrase a lot in this book because I whole-heartedly believe it to be true: Comparison is a thief. It steals. It kills. It destroys.

Now, am I saying you'll kill someone or someone will kill you if you dabble in the art of comparison? No. I doubt that will ever happen. But I do believe that we suffer greatly when we are the ones handling the measuring stick. It happens when we see our offering side by side, altar to altar, and we see the scale, just like Cain did. Sometimes the scale tips our way. Sometimes it doesn't.

In the field that day, this idea of comparing what one person has to the other began. A basket full of fruit compared to a sled full of fat. A heart that didn't care about the offering to the one who cared greatly. Not good, to good enough. The consequences were devastating. God wasn't asking Cain to compare. He was asking Cain to give his best. God wasn't comparing the offering. He was searching their hearts. What was on those altars was a representation of what was in the hearts of those two brothers. If Cain had given his best fruits with a pure heart and motive, his offering would have been acceptable. Cain is the one who compared. He's also the one who let that comparison ruin him.

From the beginning, comparison has been a thief. From the very beginning of time, comparison has disrupted lives, broken relationships, and crushed hearts. Do you see it now? Here we are over two-thousand years later and we are still battling this "apples to oranges" mentality. This should encourage you. How? Well, it's nothing new. It happened in the beginning of the world and it happened throughout the Bible as we will see in a few of the chapters in this book. Even people who God chose to put in the Bible struggled with comparison. They weren't even immune to it. At least you know you're not alone...and neither am I.

What I'm asking you to do over these next chapters is kind of tough but I know you can do it. I'm asking you to open the pages of this book and in doing so, open your heart. All of it. Every nook. Every cranny. The healthy places. The sick places. The neat places. The messy ones too. The seen places as well as the unseen. Open it all. He sees it anyway. The difference is that when we voluntarily open our hearts, we give Him permission to work. Work in us. Work through us. Work for us.

You'll have to ask yourself

> The difference is that when we voluntarily open our hearts, we give Him permission to work. Work in us. Work through us. Work for us.

some hard questions. You'll have to give some real answers. Vulnerability is scary. And hard. And worth it. So, will you do it? Not for me, even though I would be humbled for you to do so. But for Him...and even more importantly, for you. He wants to speak to you about this. About where your heart is. Comparing one of His daughters to another has never been something God desires. It goes against His "Daddy's Heart" for you, His daughter. He has more for you. So much more.

Oh, dear one, will you join me in this prayer as we walk together along this journey of revelation, restoration, and healing. "Father, I choose to open my heart to all that You have for me in the pages of this book. I desire for You to speak to the places that are hard. And messy. And scary. And hidden. Comparison has been a thief in my life for too long and I want You to help me. Give me wisdom, and courage, and strength. Thank you for loving me the way that You do. I open my heart and trust You with it. In Jesus Name, Amen."

All the Fat
Study Guide

1. What comparison did Cain make and with whom did he make it? _____

_____

_____

_____

2. Ultimately, what did this comparison cost him?

_____

_____

_____

_____

3. "He didn't lose the opportunity to be in God's presence because he compared his offering to his brothers. He lost that opportunity because he acted on the feelings that comparison brings." What feelings did comparison bring to Cain? How could he have handled it differently?

_____

_____

_____

_____

_____

4. "From the beginning, comparison has been a thief."
Explain what you think that means.

_____

_____

_____

_____

_____

Father,

In Your presence I am safe – safe from lies; safe from
condemnation; safe from self-doubt. I'm safe, also, Lord,
to see my heart the way You see it. So, here in Your
presence, I tell You, "I trust You, Father. I trust Your ways
and I trust Your kind and good heart towards me." Amen.

This prayer was written and prayed over you by one of
the spiritual giants that God kindly placed in my life,
Teresa Bishop.

The Carnage of Comparison

It would be very easy to think that we women can just walk around, comparing ourselves to each other and it not matter, right? That we can dabble in the art of comparison and there be no consequences. After all, is it *really* such a big deal? Is it *really* that harmful? Can comparison really lead to carnage of epic proportions? Oh sister, yes it can! Think of Macy's after a one-day Spring Sale where all shoes were sixty percent off and you had a coupon. Imagine, shoe boxes everywhere, heels with no matches sitting sideways on the benches, tissue paper floating in the air, women crying in the corner because they were out of size eight's. Complete carnage. Only this type of carnage isn't in the shoe store, it's displayed in the lives of women every day. Comparison is a thief and it's here to destroy you.

What is comparison, really? Well, the definition is to "examine in order to note the similarities or differences of something", or in this case, someone. That sounds harmless enough right? Me, examining another woman in order to see what similarities or what differences we have. Yep, completely harmless. Until, that is, you throw human nature into the mix, then it becomes reminiscent of the Macy's shoe department.

See, here's the thing, comparison was never meant to create such destruction in a woman's life, but the truth is, it does nothing BUT destroy. John 10:10 says, "The thief comes to steal, kill, and destroy..." Now, this verse is talking about Satan but I find it quite interesting that those three words are used to describe what Satan comes to do when comparison could say the same. Satan, the thief, has come to this earth to steal from us, kill us, and destroy us. You know what, I believe he is using the comparison game as one of his greatest tools to steal our confidence, kill our dreams, and destroy us as women. The ultimate thief is using comparison because it too, is a thief.

What makes comparison such a horrible thief? What does it kill and what does it destroy? Well, if you remember, comparison in and of itself isn't wrong and neither is the act of comparing yourself to someone else. The issue is what it leads to on the inside. It's what our hearts do with the data of the comparison. Because we are human and don't always get it right, the act of comparison stirs up

> The issue is what it leads to on the inside. It's what our hearts do with the data of the comparison.

some very negative things inside of us and then those negative things eventually come out of us. That's the idea behind comparison stealing from us. It robs us of who we are and who we can be. It steals our joy, kills our hope, and destroys our outlook. So, what exactly does comparison lead to in our lives? What negative and unhealthy fruit does it display in women? Well, the list is long and the fruit is rotten! You'll also begin to see how all of these unhealthy fruits begin to mix together, kind of like a fruit salad, only it's rotten, and no one wants to eat it...like ever.

Pride

This unattractive attribute leaks all over a woman who chooses to compare herself to someone else. Here's an example: Trudy is at her son's baseball practice and notices another mom on the bleachers. The mom's name is Leanne and she is new to the area. Trudy begins to analyze this mom in every way. What is she wearing? Does she have a designer bag? Are her nails done? Trudy then makes a conscious decision to see how she measures up to Leanne and that is where the trouble begins.

"I'm definitely skinnier than her."

"She may have a Kate Spade bag but mine is a Michael Kors and it's from his latest line."

"She didn't even pack a snack for her other child. I'm a much better mom than that!"

"She has a full time job and probably doesn't have time for her kids. She should stay home like me"

Trudy walks away from that practice feeling pretty good about herself. After all, she came out on top. She came out as the winner in the war of "which woman is better". She strolls to her car with her chin tilted upward, her proud shoulders pushed back, and her Michael Kors bag held tightly beside her. She's on top of the world and she's loving every minute of it.

As an outsider looking in, pride looks pretty ugly doesn't it? As ugly as a perm and leg warmers in the 80's. When Trudy chose to compare herself to Leanne, she put herself above that other woman. She made herself feel better by comparing all of her great qualities to someone else's not-so-great qualities.

Now, let me give you another example of pride, one that just may surprise you. A few days later, Trudy is at her daughter's band concert. Another one of the band moms, Julie, begins to walk toward her. Immediately, Trudy becomes uncomfortable. Julie is really fit, trim, and is always dressed to the "nine's". Tonight was no exception. Julie sits down and starts telling Trudy about the birthday party she was planning for her daughter. There is a band, a dance floor, several food stations, and the pool will be lit up with homemade floating candles. Julie pulls out apples and peanut butter for her youngest child, all the while sharing how she has an opportunity to lead her small group study on prayer and how it's changing her prayer life dramatically! Once the concert is over, Trudy heads back to her car, head down, shoulders slumped, and with these thoughts whirling in her head:

"She is so fit and beautiful. I could never look like that."

"I wish I could plan parties like her. Mine are always so

boring. I'm boring."

"She brought apples and peanut butter for her kids snack. I had skittles for mine. She must think I'm the worst mom ever."

"She's a much better Christian than me. I am not good enough to lead a small group."

Hello pride. You must be thinking, "Ummmm, wait Karen, that's not pride. Pride is when you think too highly of yourself or think you're better than someone else." Well, friend, you are half right. Pride is also thinking *less* of yourself. See, pride is when YOU are at the center. It is self-focused. All of your thinking is wrapped around you. It's self-absorption. Whether you think too highly of yourself or not enough of yourself. It's when you think you are all that and a bag of chips AND when you think you are chopped liver. Your thoughts are completely focused inward, on you. Self. Whether you are too good or not good

> Comparison may be a thief but pride is a liar.

enough, that's pride. Whether you can do everything right or nothing right, that's pride. Pride is any time "self" rules.

Comparison leads to pride and pride is something that God detests. Comparison may be a thief but pride is a liar. The Bible speaks about pride fifty-four times and trust me, it's never anything good. Here are just a few verses that will prove that point:

"I will break down your stubborn pride." Leviticus 26:19

"The pride of your heart has deceived you..." Obadiah 1:3

"His pride led to his downfall." 2 Chronicles 26:16

"When pride comes, then comes disgrace." Proverbs 11:2

"Pride goes before destruction, a haughty spirit before a fall." Proverbs 16:18

"God opposes the proud but shows favor to the humble." James 4:6

See, God has strong feelings about pride. We should too. I don't want God to have to break down my stubborn pride. I don't want to be deceived, experience a downfall, or be disgraced. I don't want destruction and I certainly don't want God to oppose me. However, all of this will take place if I choose pride. The pride of me thinking I am everything as well as the pride of me thinking that I am nothing. Self-absorption takes God out of the scenario. If we think we can do it all, we don't need Him. If we think we can't do anything, we've said He isn't enough. Pride exists when we focus on ourselves. Comparison makes us do just that. We turn the focus inward to what we are or what we aren't. Comparison inevitably leads to pride and pride doesn't please God.

Insecurity

Insecurity is defined as a lack of confidence or assurance and having self-doubt. It's pretty easy to see how comparison can bring forth insecurity isn't it? Remember Trudy? Well, when Trudy compared

> Self-absorption takes God out of the scenario. If we think we can do it all, we don't need Him. If we think we can't do anything, we've said He isn't enough.

herself to Julie, her insecurities began to shout in her face...and in her heart. Insecurity began its assault on Trudy's self-confidence as soon as she compared Julie's strengths to her own. Her own strengths were diminished and squashed until all that was left was Trudy's shattered self-confidence.

Sometimes insecurity is displayed when a woman constantly talks down to herself or about herself. Always doubting her talents and abilities. She tends to avoid any tasks that would make her feel inadequate in those abilities. Insecure women often cannot receive a compliment and will deflect any given. For instance, if I were to compliment her on her hair, she might say, "Well, it doesn't normally look this good, it's just a fluke. You should see it every other day, it looks terrible!" Or, I may compliment her on a dessert that she brought to small group and she says, "It was from a box. Anyone could have made it and I'm sure it could have been better." She also has difficulty looking others in the eyes. It makes her uncomfortable because she doesn't want to be seen and she knows that the eyes are the window to the soul. Insecurity can also show up in the form of people-pleasing. She has the false belief that she must please everyone and has a difficult time saying no. It makes her feel like a bad person to say no and the thought that she might let that person down is just too much to bear.

Sometimes an insecure woman is just the opposite in the way she displays her insecurity. She is loud, and dominant, and critical. Her goal is to mask her insecurity with power and sometimes a harsh personality. She tries to control the situation in such a way that people would never notice her insecurity. Sometimes she's a bully. She makes fun of other women, tearing them down with hurtful jokes. Sometimes she brags on herself, drawing attention to her strengths so no one will focus on her weaknesses. She is quick to point out flaws in other women and doesn't mind sharing those flaws with twenty-five of her closest friends.

Insecurity is the branch, but comparison is the root. Honestly, I think most women struggle with insecurity in some way. We all have that battle with self-doubt sometimes. I remember when I was asked to audition as a co-host for a TV home improvement show. I walked into the audition as a thirty-two year old mother of two who had just found out she was about to be a mother of THREE! I walked into that television studio and sat down. Then, I made the mistake of looking around. I was surrounded by twenty-two girls who were all twenty-something. They were all gorgeous...and not pregnant. I heard them all talking about their head shots and who their photographer was. I realized that they had all brought in their own head shots in portfolios. I looked down in my lap and shuddered because the only thing I had brought in was my car keys. My car keys ya'll. I immediately began to doubt myself, my abilities, where God had put me, and I wanted to leave that room so badly. I said to the Lord, "What in THE WORLD am I doing here? No one is going to cast a thirty-two year old pregnant woman for this show. Why am I even here Lord?" He spoke so gently to my racing heart, "You're here because I told you to be here. Trust Me." I got myself together the best I could, still struggling with whether I was any good at this TV thing or not, doubting, so much doubting. One by one, I watched those girls go back to the audition room and then leave out the front door. I was last. The producer called my name and I headed back to the audition room. I auditioned. They laughed. It was a good laugh. Right before I finished the audition, I went ahead and told them that I was pregnant and that I understood if that wouldn't work for their TV plans. The producer walked me to my car and told me it would be two weeks before they made a decision on the co-host. He said I wouldn't get a call if I didn't get the job. I drove home heavy, doubting my ability, doubting my decision to audition, doubting, well…doubting me. Three days passed and I got a phone call from the producer. He told me that I was everyone's first choice and offered me the job. He went on to say that I was gifted and talented and would go far. I vividly remember shooting an episode of the show when I was eight months pregnant. It was an all-male cast, except for the VERY pregnant lady and in the middle of the shoot, I began having labor pains. I've never seen a group of men so uncomfortable in my life. They were asking if I needed towels or boiling water. In the middle of breathing through the contractions, I said, "What am I supposed to do with towels and boiling water?" One of the producers said, "I have no idea...that's just what they say on TV when a woman goes into labor!"

> We all struggle with those moments of self-doubt but that doesn't mean we have to stay there.

Self-doubt and insecurity happens to all of us at times. Beth Moore says, "We all have insecurities. They piggyback on the vulnerability inherent in our humanity. The question is whether or not our insecurities are substantial enough to hurt, limit, or even distract us from profound effectiveness or fulfillment of purpose. Are they cheating us of the powerful and abundant life Jesus flagrantly promised? Do they nip at our heels all the way from the driveway to the workplace? Scripture claims that believers in Christ are enormously gifted people. Are our insecurities snuffing the Spirit until our gifts, for all practical purposes, are largely unproductive or, at the very least, tentative?" We all struggle with those moments of self-doubt but that doesn't mean we have to stay there.

Remember how I said that unhealthy fruits tend to mix together, kind of like a fruit salad? Well, here's what I mean. Beth Moore explains it like this in her book, So

Long, Insecurity; you've been a bad friend to us, "As long as we live, our self-absorption and our insecurity will walk together, holding hands and swinging them back and forth like two little girls on their way to a pretend playground they can never find. Human nature dictates that most often we will be as insecure as we are self-absorbed." It seems as if one bad fruit breeds another. Pride and insecurity seem to go together like peanut butter and jelly, but this is one sandwich I don't want to take a bite of!

Weak Female Relationships

Another byproduct of comparison is weak female relationships. A woman who has a tendency to compare herself to other women will often find herself alone. Not necessarily because she WANTS to be alone, but because that is the cost of constant comparison in her life. Think about it, if she is constantly comparing herself to other women and she's the one that comes up short, does she really want to hang out with those women and feel the weight of not measuring up? Nope. No way. So, she distances herself from anyone who would make her feel "less-than". She feels as if she can deal with being alone more easily than she can deal with the weight of feeling like a failure as a woman. When I encounter a woman who tells me that she just doesn't have any female friends, my red flag goes up immediately. That may not always be the case when a woman lacks female friendships, but it can be. She doesn't want to lose at the game of comparison so she never lets anyone in her life to compare herself to. Her relationships with other women are weak, and shallow and she prefers it that way. It hurts less. It's less work. It's less everything.

A woman who struggles with comparison will also push other women away. Several years ago, a young woman and I became friends. We had several things in common and our friendship was pretty easy, or so I thought. Then, things began to change. She began to distance herself from me. At the time, I wasn't really sure what was happening. I continued to reach out, be kind, and pursue our friendship. I began hearing from other people that she was saying some very mean things about me. I was hurt and I didn't understand. I called her and asked her if the things I was hearing was true. She said that it was true and then proceeded to tell me everything that she saw that was wrong with me. How horrible of a person I was. That I was fake. How the sight of me made her sick. I told her that I was sorry she felt that way and I truly was. She hung up and I cried. And cried. I was heartbroken. Her words cut deeper than a sharpened sword ever could. What I thought was a good friendship was obviously not healthy and it vanished right before my eyes. As I began to seek counsel on my situation, the consensus was the same and it boiled down to these three things: she had a problem with comparison; she had jealousy issues; and she chose to push me away. Even to this day, this young woman does not have strong female relationships. If she considers another woman a threat, competition, or comparison, she won't befriend that woman. She has had difficulty building strong, deep female relationships because of her insecurity. Once again, these rotten fruits overlap and go hand in hand. It's sad. My heart hurts for her and I have prayed for her for years. I've prayed that she would allow God to swoop in and heal her heart. I'm trusting that He will. I know He is able and I know He can. Weak female relationships and the act of pushing other women away is a sign that comparison has taken its toll.

Jealousy and Envy

Jealousy is defined as being hostile toward a rival or one believed to enjoy an advantage. Envy is defined as painful or resentful awareness of an advantage enjoyed by another joined with a desire to possess the same advantage. These two are buddies. They too, walk hand in hand. Just look at some of the words listed in both definitions: hostile, rival, painful, resentful, possess. Such sweet words aren't they? These words speak to the depravity of a heart when comparison has rule and reign.

One example in the Bible of how jealousy played a devastating part in two lives is the story of Saul and David. Saul was the youngest in the tribe of Benjamin and was anointed king by the prophet Samuel. He was king for some time and then he disobeyed God. God took His hand off of Saul but he continued sitting on the king's throne. Meanwhile, God had told Samuel to anoint a new king, a son of Jesse. His name was David and he was a shepherd. Saul and David's path crossed when Saul needed someone to play the harp for him. They built a friendship and all was well. David became a warrior, a leader, and made a name for himself in the city. And then one day, one simple phrase changed it all. Saul and David had just arrived back into town from a battle they had won and the women began lining the streets and broke out the tambourines, harps, and cymbals. Talk about a welcome home party! Within the excitement of the victory and the pride of winning a battle, one phrase tore it all to the ground. The women began singing, "Saul has slain his thousands, and David his tens of thousands." (1 Samuel 18:7) Ouch. Double ouch. Saul hadn't compared himself to David, other people had, and he had come up short. This sent Saul into a rage and on several occasions he attempted to kill David. Why? Because Saul was jealous and envious of David's advantage,

> Remember, it's not the actual act of comparison that is the issue, it's what we do with the data after the comparison has been made that is the problem. It's what happens on the inside.

his favor, his success. The comparison that was made literally made Saul want to end David's life. Remember, it's not the actual act of comparison that is the issue, it's what we do with the data after the comparison has been made that is the problem. It's what happens on the inside. On the inside, Saul took the women's song and replayed it over and over again in his head. The jealousy burned within him and it eventually destroyed Saul.

Jealousy can show up anywhere. In the workplace, in families, in friendships, in acquaintances, in churches,

> Jealousy invades and envy slays

at ball games, at the grocery store, at a play date...just about anywhere. Jealousy invades and envy slays. This is the ugly fruit that comparison grows. Do you remember the definition of jealousy and envy? It is being hostile toward a rival or one believed to enjoy an advantage. Envy is defined as painful or resentful awareness of an advantage enjoyed by another joined with a desire to possess the same advantage. First of all, why do we have to consider one another rivals? Why can't we think of one another as a person? We ladies are all walking the same life journey on this same planet at the same time, so let's be each other's cheerleaders instead of acting like we are all on opposite teams! Ladies, we are not rivals, do you hear me...we are NOT rivals. That definition says that jealousy is being hostile to someone who has an advantage. What that really means is that when something good happens to someone, we don't like it. We don't want it to happen. Envy goes on to say that not only do we dislike that something good happened but we want that something good to happen to us too. Craig Groeschel said, "Envy is resenting God's goodness in someone else's life and ignoring His own goodness in your life."

Girls...we need to clap for each other when we win! Denise Smith, a beautiful soul and the author of Seeds of Purpose penned this and I wholeheartedly agree. "It's a sign of maturity and enlightenment to be supportive, gratefully encouraged...and even excited--when we witness others enjoying their moments of comfort and celebration." I like how she purposely adds the word "maturity" to her thoughts. Why? Because I find that the women who are growing in their maturity in the Lord are so much more willing to applaud other women than those who are not. Zen Shin said, "A flower does not think of competing with the flower next to it. It just blooms." How about some blooming support huh? You go ahead and bloom and let the flower next to you do the same. Now, that will make one beautiful flower garden won't it?

Pride, insecurity, weak female relationships, jealousy and envy...what a list huh? This, my friends, is what comparison leads to in the hearts of every woman who participates in this game, this comparison trap. Maybe not all of them will find a home in a woman's heart but you can bet your bottom dollar that at least one of those rotten fruits will find its way in and continue to rot. You might be thinking, "But Karen, I would never allow those things in my heart to take up residence!" I understand your thinking, I really do, but here's the problem, that rotten fruit is an unintended consequence of comparison. We might not set out with the intention of housing those bad fruits but that is why comparison is such a sneaky thief. We may set out to simply note how we are similar or different from "her" but remember, comparison in and of itself is not the issue, it's what we do with the data we find within the comparison

> Comparison is not just a slippery slope. It is, without a doubt, a dangerous downhill landslide.

that makes it all go south. When we choose to compare, we are letting one of those nasty fruits in, to invade, to set up camp, and to possibly breed more bad fruit. Comparison is not just a slippery slope. It is, without a doubt, a dangerous downhill landslide.

When we choose to compare ourselves to others, there is a great cost. A cost that could never be calculated by money, but instead by loss. Deep loss. Tragic loss. That loss steals our self -worth. It kills our kindness. It destroys our destiny. Just like Satan wants to do. There is great carnage at the hands of comparison, similar to that of the Macy's shoe store. The biggest difference is that we are not fighting for shoes...we are fighting for our lives.

The Carnage of Comparison
Study Guide

1. What is comparison?

_____

_____

_____

2. Is comparison a bad thing? Explain

_____

_____

_____

3. What negative and unhealthy fruit does comparison produce in us?

a. _____

b. _____

c. _____ __ _____

d. _____ & _____

4. Write down your thoughts about the Carnage of Comparison.

_____

_____

_____

_____

Father God,

Thank You that You have made each one of us
uniquely. Thank You that You have liberally given each
of us a different blend of talents, gifts and abilities. And,
Father, we know that we have an enemy who has come to
steal, kill and destroy, but Jesus has come to give us
life…a life we can live to the full. A life fully lived using
the abilities that You've graced us with. But, we can't
abundantly live if we are constantly comparing ourselves
with other women. So Father, in Your Son's name, I pray
against pride, insecurity, jealousy and envy in the hearts
of each of the women reading this today. I ask that in this
moment, Your Holy Spirit would reveal those areas in
which comparison is getting the best of them. Those
moments where pride and insecurity have robbed them of
joy. Where jealousy and envy have stolen potentially
meaningful relationships from them. I pray that their
eyes would be open to Your goodness in their life. May
they choose from this day forward to celebrate and
applaud the successes of others without belittling the
good things that You have done in and through them.
May they remember that You began a good work and You
intend to complete it…in ALL Your children. We ask all
these things, thanking you again for the way You

intricately knit each one of us, in Your Son's precious name, Jesus!

This prayer was written and prayed over you by my beautiful and precious friend, Terri Torbett.

Liar, Liar, Pants on Fire!

Just one time, ONE TIME, I'd like to see a liar's pants actually catch on fire. What a sight that would be huh? We'd all know who the liars of the world were because they'd all be walking around with fiery britches! Here's the thing, there's one, big, fat liar whose pants are eternally in flames. You might think he'd be easy to spot, walking around with his pants on fire and all, but he's an exceptionally sly liar. He's my enemy. He's your enemy too. 1 Peter 5:8 gives us a warning. "Be self-controlled and alert. Your enemy the devil prowls around like a roaring lion looking for someone to devour."

How do I know that this enemy, the devil, is a liar? Well, all you have to do is ask Eve, she'll tell you. She got lied to by a sneaky, slithery serpent. This serpent is also the lion that was talked about in 1 Peter. Our enemy is Satan. And he is a liar.

In Genesis 2:16-17, God warns of one rule concerning the Garden of Eden. "And the LORD God commanded the man, 'You are free to eat from any tree in the garden; but you must not eat from the tree of the knowledge of good and evil, for when you eat of it you will surely die.'" Then that sneaky, sly, slithery serpent shows up. Genesis 3:1 "Now the serpent was more crafty than any of the wild animals the LORD God had made. He said to the woman, 'Did God really say, 'You must not eat from any tree in the garden?'" See just how crafty he was, and not like Hobby Lobby crafty either, just plain old sneaky crafty. That serpent knew exactly what God had said. That suggestive, "Did God really say" allowed Eve to second guess what she heard. Doubt it. Question it. Her response? "The woman said to the serpent, 'We may eat fruit from the trees in the garden, but God did say, "You must not eat fruit from the tree that is in the middle of the garden, and you must not touch it, or you will die."'" Genesis 3:2-3 Poor Eve. I wonder if she ever stood a chance against that snake-like lion. The one that was seeking to devour her. She seemed a bit confused didn't she? She added on the part about God saying not to touch the fruit. He never said that. The snake goes in for the kill like the lion he is. "You will not surely die," the serpent said to the woman. "For God knows that when you eat of it your eyes will be opened, and you will be like God, knowing good and evil." Genesis 3:4-5. Satan insinuates that God is purposely withholding something good from Eve. That was it for Eve. It was all she needed to make her choice. She was toast. And she was about to get some fruit to spread on that toast! Genesis 3:16-7 "When the woman saw that the fruit of the tree was good for food and pleasing to the eye, and also desirable for gaining wisdom, she took some and ate it. She also gave some to her husband, who was with her, and he ate it. Then the eyes of both of them were opened, and they realized they were naked..."

Eve got what she wanted, or at least what she thought she wanted. God confronts her in verse 13, "Then the LORD God said to the woman, 'What is this you have done?' and Eve replies, 'The serpent deceived me, and I ate.'" So nooooowwww you realize he's a deceiver Eve? Sigh. If only she had had that bit of insight a few minutes earlier we wouldn't need epidurals during labor. Thanks Eve. Thanks a lot.

So, why this long story of Eve and the liar? What does it have to do with you or me? Well, let me just say this, Eve ain't the only woman that old serpent has been lying to. He's been lying to you too. Oh, trust me, he's been lying to me for years as well. We've been duped my friend, duped I tell you! Unfortunately, this story of a serpent lying to a lady in a perfect garden set a precedence in the spiritual realm. This opened a gateway for the enemy to think that he had every right to lie to us, and that we, as women, would just have to believe him. That first lie spoken to Eve set in motion thousands of years of detestable whispers into the souls of women. Lies that have held us captive. Lies that have decimated our self-esteem. Lies that have ripped at the very fabric of our core. When Satan chose to destroy Eve that day, he chose to destroy all women. You. Me. Every

> This opened a gateway for the enemy to think that he had every right to lie to us, and that we, as women, would just have to believe him. That first lie spoken to Eve set in motion thousands of years of detestable whispers into the souls of women.

woman. That day in the Garden, a war was waged on our hearts. That moment in time opened a door that we need to shut. I don't know about you girl, but I intend to shut that door today. Are you with me?

Do you know the best thing that can happen to a liar? Well, besides his pants actually catching on fire. The best thing that can happen to a liar is having his lies exposed. Hooking him up to a lie-detector machine and watching him sweat. So that's what we are going to do. We are going to shed some light on the lies our enemy whispers to us in the night. We are going to call out the lies that he shouts at us when we are alone. We are going to make that liar and his pants pay for deceiving us all these years.

Satan is the author of all lies. Every lie we've ever believed originated with him. Now, you may have heard someone shout some of these lies at you. You may have cried as someone who you thought loved you spouted off these lies and they seeped into your soul. YOU may have even spoken some of these lies to yourself in the stillness of the night. But know this. It was him. It's always him. The crafty serpent who twists words and causes confusion. The sneaky snake who insinuates that God is up to no good. The deceiver himself. The lion who crouches low, waiting to pounce and devour his unsuspecting prey. Think I'm being too hard on him? Wait until you hear the lies he's been feeding you all these years. You'll want to set his pants on fire yourself, trust me.

*You are not worthy of love.

*You don't deserve anything good in your life.

*You are ugly.

*You aren't good at anything.

*You will never amount to anything.

*No one will ever want you.

*Things will never get better.

*You'll always be alone.

*There's nothing special about you.

*Your past is not redeemable.

*No one would miss you if you were gone.

*Things will never change.

Here's a match. Light him up. And ya'll, these are only SOME of the lies he spews at us. How many of these lies have you believed about yourself? Whether they were spoken to you or you spoke them over yourself, they are lies, all lies. Here's the hard part. Once you heard these lies, you then took ownership of them and made them a part of who you are by believing them. These lies play over and over in your head like a taped recording, looping the lies over and over again. That recording just keeps playing in your head and your heart like a broken record. These lies steal the joy and the purpose from your life. They beat you down, day after day. These lies are relentless. And consuming. And believable.

Here's what I've also noticed. When you believe the recording in your head, it becomes the filter in which you see life. Everything that happens to you, you see through the lens of those lies. For example, your boss comes to you and tells you that you are up for a promotion at your job. He says he'll let you know Monday if you will be getting the new position. Your first reaction in your head is something like, "Well, it sounds really good but I probably won't get the promotion. Sarah should get it because she is better at her job than me anyway." The lens in which you see life has been tainted with the lie, "You don't

> When you believe the recording in your head, it becomes the filter in which you see life. Everything that happens to you, you see through the lens of those lies.

deserve anything good in your life." That's the filter in which you see everything that happens to you.

Another example would be if your friends make a huge fuss over you for your birthday. They throw you a surprise party and invite all of your closest friends. As you begin reading the birthday cards they have given you, most of them are filled with encouraging phrases like, "You are one of a kind!", "I'm so glad you are my friend!", "You are so special to me!", and "My life wouldn't be the same without you!". You immediately think to yourself, "Well, they have to say those things to me, it's my birthday." The lens, or the filter in which you see your life through are the lies, "There's nothing special about you" and "You are not worthy of love."

These are only two examples but they show just how destructive these lies are. They skew everything. Every circumstance, situation, or relationship is colored by the lies we've allowed to make a home in our hearts.

> The enemy whispered the lies, but we let them find a resting place in our hearts.

The enemy whispered the lies, but we let them find a resting place in our hearts. We let them set up camp within us. They are like the lenses in

the glasses of life that we can never remove. Until today.
Today we take off those lenses to see the truth. That's
how we combat the lies, with truth. Real Truth. Truth
from the very Word of God. This is what the Lord says
about you, beloved.

*You are fearfully and wonderfully made.
Psalm 139:14

*You are engraved in the palm of His hand.
Isaiah 49:16

*You are the apple of His eye. Zechariah 2:8

*You are His treasured possession.
Deuteronomy 7:6

*You are precious, honored, and loved by Him.
Isaiah 43:4

*You are redeemed. He calls you by name. You are
His. Isaiah 43:1

*You are chosen. 1 Peter2:9

Girl, this is what Truth looks like! This is the knowledge
of the Lord, what we know of Him to be true. This is the
recording that needs to be looping in your head and
heart! Doesn't this sound so much better than the bowl
full of lies that jerk of a snake Satan feeds you? 2
Corinthians 10:5 says, "We demolish arguments and
every pretension that sets itself up against the knowledge
of God, and we take captive every thought to make it

obedient to Christ." The word "pretension" here means "claims". So, we can say that we destroy arguments, or in this case, destroy lies, and every claim that Satan has made that goes against what we know about God, and we will choose to dwell on His truths instead of Satan's lies. All those truths listed above? That is the knowledge of God. That is what we know of the truth of our God. This is how we take off those glasses with the jacked-up filter. This is how we stop that loop of lies from replaying in our heart. This is how we kick the lies out from making a home in our hearts. Those lies can't set up camp within us. Nope. No camping allowed here. No more lies. No more snake. No more lion. Just truth.

We've spent a whole chapter talking about our enemy, the devil. Now that you know it was him lying to you all these years, do you wonder why? Why would Satan take the time to impart these lies to you? Why would he make the effort? Doesn't he have better things to do like trying to put out his fire-laden pants? Well, the enemy is no dummy. He knows that if he keeps feeding women these lies, we will be bound up in shackles. A blogger wrote on her blog, "Desiring Rain", "Women today are bombarded with more and more lies from Satan. There is almost an epidemic of "soul-sickness" and it is not just among women in the world but also among those of us in church. Why? Because Satan wants us in bondage. He wants both you and me not to live freely but rather to live under a cloud of personal guilt and condemnation. He doesn't want us to enjoy the grace and love of God so he whispers lies to us. During our walk, we may stir up a lot of religious dust but we won't do Satan's kingdom any real damage when we listen and dwell on his lies." Bondage. That's where he wants us. We will be imprisoned, standing behind the bars of what we aren't so as to never discover what we are. If we chew on the lies, we can never swallow the Truth and the Truth is what will set us free. It is his hope that with every lie women believe, they will be distracted, preoccupied, busy,

> We will be imprisoned, standing behind the bars of what we aren't so as to never discover what we are.

and beat down. So much so that we sit down. We give up. We throw our shackled hands in the air in surrender. The further he keeps us from the Truth, the better. Did you notice what the writer of the blog was saying? She shared that when we believe his lies and are in bondage, we are of no real threat to Satan or his kingdom. The idea being that we may "stir up a lot of religious dust" but nothing of significance will be done to battle the enemy. Nothing will be done of great impact to demolish and destroy Satan's domain. It's not that we don't want to, it's that we CAN'T. We can't wield a sword with our hands in shackles. We can't stand firm if we are cowering in the corner, believing we aren't capable of anything. We can't speak victory over the powers of darkness when our mouths are silenced with disbelief. It's Satan's mightiest tool in his toolbox. In fact, if Satan had a written game plan, a strategy for his demons to see, it would look like this: "Keep them distracted with who they aren't. Keep them embarrassed with who they are. Keep them squashed with fear and shackled with shame. Help them believe the worst about themselves. That they can't. That they won't. That they shouldn't. Keep them in bondage to the lies and they'll be stuck. Stuck is good. Crushed is even better. I win, they lose. Those women won't even know what hit 'em."

See, he doesn't want you to read this book. He doesn't want you to share this book. He doesn't want you to grow from this book. It scares him. It should. Think of the truths in this book as a sword. It was a hidden sword until today and you didn't even know it existed. But, now you do. This knowledge, this Truth, is the sword that will cut the head off that snake and will puncture through the heart of that ferocious lion. Psalm 91:13 calls out this Truth. "You will tread upon the lion and the cobra: you will trample the great lion and the serpent." The chains and the shackles are off, and so are the boxing gloves, and you have declared the enemy dead to you.

You are now equipped, my warrior friend, to combat any lie with the sword of Truth. Satan doesn't get to lie to you anymore. You've called his bluff. You know his game. You smell his smoky pants.

> This knowledge, this Truth, is the sword that will cut the head off that snake and will puncture through the heart of that ferocious lion.

Liar, Liar, Pants on Fire
Study Guide

1. What happened to Eve in the garden?

_____

_____

_____

_____

2. What lies listed in this chapter have you believed about yourself? Are there any other lies not listed that you allow to "loop" in your head?

_____

_____

_____

_____

3. What should you combat Satan's lies with? List some of the ones that spoke to you.

_____

_____

_____

_____

4. Now that you know Satan's tactics and his lies, how

will this change the way you do life?

_____

_____

_____

_____

_____

Abba Father,

You are so, so good! You spoke into the void and there
was light! You created the heavens and the earth, you
breathed life into a lump of clay! You are all-knowing,
all-powerful, creator, and yet you call us your daughters.
You love with an everlasting love, from creation you
made a way for us to commune with you! Thank you for
your word, your truth written upon our hearts. Help us
to use that truth to combat the enemy's fiery darts, those
darts of fear, doubt, insecurity, shame. Your daughter's
are being attacked, Satan is winning the battle, he's
binding us up in in shackles of unworthiness and fear.
Father, help us to see that although Satan may be winning
the battle YOU have already won the war! I pray that
through these words freedom will come, freedom from
unrealistic expectations, freedom from shame, freedom
from guilt, freedom from looking at others' highlights and

feeling as if we fall short! Father, strengthen your child, fill her with your presence. You stood outside of time and you chose this moment, this book in your daughter's hand, knowing the brokenness, knowing the circumstances that feel so unbearable, her hurts, her fears, her insecurities, her pain and you love her still, she is the apple of your eye! Father you knit her together in her mother's womb. You have a purpose and a plan for her life! Give her a boldness to STAND up! Give her a boldness to tell the enemy NO MORE! Give her the courage to speak truth to the lies the enemy taunts her with. Father, help her to see herself as you see her. Your beloved! Strong mighty warrior princess, the enemy quakes with fear at the thought of her rising up to be who you created her to be. He intimidates, knowing, if she glimpses who she really is in you, she will be unstoppable for your kingdom! Let these words pierce through the scars, pierce through the strongholds, let them hit the heart, let them awaken what has been sleeping, let them awaken the fierceness that you tucked in her soul at the time of creation.

In Jesus Name,

Amen!

This prayer was written and prayed over you by my friend and mighty prayer warrior, Mary Hanson.

Enough IS Enough!

Here's a word for ya..."enough". Actually, two words, "not enough". Ever felt like that? Like you were just not enough? Here are a few real life stories of young women who have felt the weight of those two words.

Helen – "Every day I look into the mirror and tell myself I am not good enough. Sometimes I think I am too young to be thinking in such ways (after all I am only twelve) but another thing inside of me tells me I MUST be thin. I can't starve myself because I can't focus in school and my mom always watches me to make sure (even though I already have). A lot of times I hate myself because I am way too ugly and my mom won't even let me put on a little foundation to cover it up. She also complains whenever I work out! Sometimes I just wish I could change everything about me. I also wish I had the guts to cut myself. So...help?"

Joy – "So, the truth is...I hate myself! I can easily hide my feelings with my personality, so no one would ever dream that I am SUPER insecure! Sometimes I even fool myself! So, my problem is exactly what Hannah wrote about. I feel like my life is a constant struggle to please EVERYONE and be miss perfect in everyone's eyes. I want more than anything to be accepted...unfortunately...by everyone! I always seem to be second best at everything. I guess a way to put it is that I am a "B" kind of person. I always seem to be "behind the scenes". My friends always think I am too this, or not good enough at that. They are never mean about anything, but every little thing gets to me hard! I am constantly comparing myself to others and it makes me depressed and angry!!!!! Then there is my family, and God. Every time I sin, or disobey my parents, I get down about it. I end up dwelling on what I did wrong, and it's like adding another heavy stone in my "back pack of life" I think my life motto right now is, "I can't do it good enough, so why even try". I know this is wrong but I can't help it!! I feel like my parents are always unhappy with me, (which isn't true), and now, I even feel like God is always unhappy with me. I feel like He doesn't hear my prayers! I KNOW for a fact that this isn't true, but I can't get rid of the feelings!!! Do you have any advice, or anything I could read or listen to that would help encourage me?"

Hanna – "Hi. My name's Hanna and I daily struggle with the idea that I'm not perfect. I constantly compare myself to my friends and to the people I see on TV. I'm never good enough for myself. I swim competitively and I'm always comparing myself to my fellow team mates and to what I think I should be at. My parents are always telling me that I shouldn't be disappointed with my swims but I can't help it. I feel that if I don't drop time every time, that I'm letting people down. It's really hard because this makes swim meets not enjoyable at all. My looks are also an issue. I feel that I'm never pretty enough or whatever and it's hard because I've never been a real girly girl but now all of a sudden I seem to care what I look like and it's just very different. Could someone help me?"

Helen, Joy, and Hanna shared their struggle and their hearts about not being enough. How it weighs on them. How it affects them. These were young ladies and they are already struggling with the "not enough's" of their life. After all, isn't that where most of us started feeling that way anyway, when we were young? Pile another thirty years or so on those stories and you have a glimpse of what many of us women are dealing with. The struggle is real and the struggle is hard, very hard.

Below is a list of just some of our "not enough's".

*I'm not good enough.

*I'm not pretty enough.

*I'm not thin enough.

*I'm not smart enough.

*I'm not happy enough.

*I'm not tall enough.

*I'm not funny enough.

*I'm not creative enough.

*I'm not a good enough wife.

*I'm not a good enough mom.

*I'm not a good enough cook.

*I'm not a good enough employee.

*I'm not a good enough friend.

*I'm not a good enough boss.

*I'm not a good enough Christian.

*I'm not a good enough worshiper.

What a list. There's probably more but I'll just stop there...I've had enough of the "not enough's". What causes us to feel this way? What is at the root of our "not enough's"? It's the same thing Cain struggled with as he weighed in on his sacrifice in relation to his little brother's. Comparison. Comparison causes the "not enough's" in our lives. When we compare our self to

> ## Comparison causes the "not enough's" in our lives.

another person, we get tackled with the "not enough's" like a quarterback who's center didn't do his job. (That football reference was for all the ladies reading who actually really like football...goooooo Dawgs, Sic 'em!) Remember, comparison is a thief. The definition of what it means to "Compare" is actually to estimate, measure, or note the similarity or dissimilarity between two things. You know, to compare apples to apples or oranges to oranges. But what happens when we compare apples to oranges?

THE FACEBOOK FALSIES

I actually like Facebook. I like it for a lot of reasons. I like it because I've been able to reconnect with people I never thought I would get to. I like it because I get to see pictures of my friends and family that I wouldn't normally get to see. I like it because I get to see what you people had for lunch. And let's just be real here, I like it because it asks me what is on my mind and most people would never be brave enough to do that. But I don't like ALL of Facebook. I don't like what it's done to us as women.

Facebook allows us to see into people's lives right? Well, sort of. Facebook gives us access but the name on the profile page is in charge of what we see. That is the person who gets to choose the cover photo and profile picture. That is the person who gets to "okay" the photos on her page. That is the person who gets to edit and re-edit what her status says. So, yes, we see into her life, but only what she wants us to see. She could be a Facebook Falsie for all we know. You know, someone who's Facebook page is picture perfect but her real life is nowhere close.

Here's why this Facebook phenomena is so tricky. We are comparing our every day to someone's highlight reel. Know what I mean? I'll never forget one day when I was stalking, I mean, ummm, looking up a lady on Facebook. She was a "friend" of mine which means I actually never met her but she friend requested me and we had 5 friends in common so I accepted. Anyway, I was checking out all of her photos and they were all amazing. There wasn't one bad picture in the bunch. In fact, their family photo was picture perfect. All of them matched. Turquoise was the color of choice, accented with coral on the girls and dark brown on the boys. The smiling little girl had a bow to match her socks, which matched her brother's bow tie. Not an out-of-place hair in sight. I threw up a little in my mouth. All I could think of is how lucky we all are in my family to leave the house with pants on most days, let alone matching socks. I felt it. The shame of not matching in our Easter pictures. The idea that somehow, our family didn't measure up because we don't own anything that matches. Not good enough because I didn't take the time to buy matching clothes. Not good enough because I didn't hire a real photographer and the picture was actually from my phone and was blurry. Not good enough.

Do you know what I did next? I took a good, hard look at my Facebook page and guess what I found out. Just like Matchy-Matchy Lady, I was a Facebook Falsie too. I didn't have one picture on there that I didn't "approve" first. There wasn't a picture of me without any makeup like when I first wake up and my hair is a hot mess and I have death breath. Not one. No posts of me being completely crazy and losing my marbles on one of my kids. Nope. There were only things on that page that I WANTED you to see, that I WANTED you to know about me. HashtagFacebookFalsie.

That is the danger of comparing our normal, everyday lives with someone else's highlight reel. It's what they want you to know or see, but maybe not who they really are. The problem is that we don't always know that, so we compare. And when we compare, we come to the conclusion that we, in some way, are not enough. It's not apples to apples. It's more like apples to monkeys. There really isn't any way to make a right comparison...so don't. Just don't. Stalk, sorry, I mean, look at their pages all you want, just look at them through the eyes of someone who understands that the highlight reel is on display. Now, as for me, I've decided not to delete my Facebook page just yet...I just HAVE to know what ya'll are having for lunch today! Hashtagyummy.

THE PINTEREST PROBLEM

Houston, we have a problem, a Pinterest problem. I was trying to figure out a way to explain what Pinterest is to those of you who may not know. It was tougher than I thought! The only way I could halfway explain it was like this; "Pinterest is a place that makes your child's last birthday party look like a toddler planned instead of an actual adult." Or how about, "Pinterest is where you go to feel creative even though you've really been sitting at your computer for the last three hours." Or this one,

"Pinterest: Where women go to plan imaginary weddings, dress children that don't exist, and decorate homes we can't afford." Makes you want to sign right up doesn't it?

Actually, Pinterest, if used well, is a great resource for all things. From the best way to get stains out of your clothes, to how to make the most delicious Prime Rib, to choosing the best eyeshadow for your eyes, and even how to make the cutest little birdseed ornaments. All really good stuff. There's just one teensy, weensy, little problem. Pinterest has an amazing talent of making us feel like absolute failures. Pinterest is the epitome of the "not-good-enoughs". Whether it's with an actual Pinterest Fail (which is where you do what Pinterest shows you, but yours turns out to be a hideous mess) or when you show up to your child's Halloween class party and you and another mom were assigned cupcakes. You bring the regular yellow cupcakes with chocolate icing. She brings the Pinterest version. Yellow cupcakes that have now morphed into spiders, complete with eight edible legs and little eyes made out of white icing and mini M&M's. Your kid looks up at you like, "Seriously mom, you couldn't do any better than that? SHE brought SPIDER CUPCAKES!" I would like to think that there is a way to live in this Pinterest world without feeling like our ideas, projects, and outfits are not good enough. I bet Pinterest has a "pin" for that!

In the world of Facebook and Pinterest, comparisons loom and holler at us "You're just not good enough!" So, why? Why do we dabble in the art of comparison? Why do we put ourselves through it? Well, we compare because we all want to know if we measure up. We want to know on a sliding scale, exactly where we stand. Or not stand. We want to evaluate our own abilities and performance. But, in the absence of objective information about our performance, we will compare ourselves to others to see how we stack up. Meaning, if someone won't tell us how we are doing in life, we'll just measure ourselves against so-and-so and see for ourselves. Are there people doing it better than me? Are there people doing it worse than me? Am I somewhere in the middle? On a scale from 1-10, am I a 6ish? Galatians 6:4-5 (TLB) says, "Let everyone be sure to do his very best, for then he will have the personal satisfaction of work done well and won't need to compare himself with someone else. Each of us must bear some faults and burdens of his own. For none of us is perfect!"

> We compare because we all want to know if we measure up.

Hmmmmm...is this verse suggesting that I just do my very best for my own personal satisfaction of a job well done and then I won't NEED to compare myself to Matchy-Matchy Lady? That's what it looks like it's saying to me. What a concept. You do your best and I'll do mine. Sometimes my best is a pot roast with gravy, served with green beans, mashed potatoes, and homemade peach cobbler for dinner. Sometimes my best is cereal...and not even the name brand kind, the generic kind. The kind where there is supposed to be an orange tiger saying, "Grrreat!" but instead it's yellow lion saying, "Niiiice!". Sometimes my best is little Nutter Butter ghosts, dipped in

> Galatians 6:4-5 (TLB) says, "Let everyone be sure to do his very best, for then he will have the personal satisfaction of work done well and won't need to compare himself with someone else. Each of us must bear some faults and burdens of his own. For none of us is perfect!"

white chocolate with mini chocolate chips for the eyes for my son's school party. Sometimes my best is store-bought sugar cookies with pink sprinkles on top. See what I'm saying? If you give your best, whatever that may look like that day, you'll be satisfied with you. What you did or didn't do. What you tried or didn't try. What you baked or didn't bake. What that Scripture is saying is that we don't need to go through our life trying to find a measuring stick. We don't need a sliding scale. We don't need to rate ourselves. If you shoot for your best, that measuring stick shatters. If you do what you can do for that day, that sliding scale crumbles. It matters not what "she" does, or "they" do. It only matters what you do. This eliminates the "not enoughs" from our lives. If we stop comparing, we stop feeling like we are not enough. Enough is enough, wouldn't you say?

Enough IS Enough
Study Guide

1. What causes us to feel like we are not good enough?

_____

_____

_____

_____

2. Explain the idea that when we compare ourselves to someone, especially on Facebook, we are comparing our every day with their highlight reel.

_____

_____

_____

_____

3. Have you ever had one of those Pinterest Fails? What happened?

_____

_____

_____

_____

_____

4. How does Galatians 6:4-5 free you up when dealing with comparison?

_____

_____

_____

_____

Wow what a chapter! Think about the word enough for just a minute. Enough means occurring in such a quantity, quality or scope as to fully meet the needs or expectation of a situation or simply put, to be adequate. My hope and prayer for you as you've completed this chapter and the study questions is that you have found yourself to be enough in the eyes of God; notice I said the eyes of God, not man. Oh my friend, I pray that you understand and know that you are fearfully and wonderfully made in His image and in the likeness of your Father. He designed you, molded you and fashioned you to be who you are. There is no one like you; no one to compare you to. Oh dear one, don't you see, He broke the mold when He made you because He made you to be enough. You are adequate to handle every situation God allows you to be placed in. The Abba Father hand crafted your looks, your attitude, and your personality to be enough for Him and to fulfill what He has planned for your life, not someone else. As I pray over you I want you to get this in your heart, let it invade your spirit. I want you to see yourself as The Father sees you. You are His cherished one, the apple of His eye and He knows you. He doesn't see you as being perfect and having it all together like you want to believe. He sees your struggles. He sees your sees your hurt and disappointment when you compare yourself to others and he wants you to know He is enough and He can cover all that and your mishaps, mistakes and mess-ups. He sees the real you, not the comparison you that others see and He is saying to you, "I am enough and I love you right where you are but I love you enough not to leave you there". Oh sister, he is asking you to pour out all your imperfection, comparisons, doubts and fears on Him so He can prove to you that you are enough for Him and He is more than enough for you. My hearts cry for you as I pray is that you allow those words [Enough Is Enough] to settle in your spirit. I pray you realize you can't compare yourself to the unrealistic expectations of others and expect to win, but that you know you can meet the expectation of The Father if you allow Him to be enough in your life. When enough is enough, will you lay down the comparison game and let God show you who you truly are? You are capable and able of being enough for your family, for your friends, for yourself and for the kingdom of God. He wants the real authentic "you", not the made up, compared to, "you". My continued prayer is that you realize you are enough because He has made you to be enough.

This prayer was written and prayed over you by my precious friend and ministry warrior, Sarah Register.

Me vs. Me

This is the chapter where I get to poor out my guts about where I am with this comparison trap. This is where I've been living. Real and messy. Often real messy. So, I hope you're ready...I'm not even sure I'm ready...but here we go anyway.

Growing up, I had my share of comparison. I could look around and see those who were prettier than me, smarter than me, better athletes than me, etc. However, for the most part, I kept a healthy balance. I found my worth, my value, and my confidence in the Lord early on, which I find to be such a gift and miracle. This gift has served me well through the years. I'm super quick to try and avoid the comparison game...because I know that some days I will feel amazing about myself and who I am and some days I will feel terrible about those same things. So, I don't play. Don't get me wrong, I still have those moments. The moments where when I see a girl with really tight skin on her thighs, I want to cover my own road-mapped, crepey, ashy thighs with a towel...and then trip her. Or when I see a gal who is really, really tiny eating a brownie sundae while I'm chewing on a carrot stick, I have to be sure not to pray that the cherry doesn't get caught in her throat. See, I have those moments too. I have to work hard to not participate sometimes because it is a natural draw in all of us, but I've been around long enough to know when I'm about to head the way of comparison. So, I can imagine you're thinking, "Then how in the world is she going to pour out her guts about something she doesn't battle?" Oh, sweet friend, I never said I didn't battle it. I battle it just about every day. And not only do I battle it, but I am the current reigning champion....of losing.

It's the battle of Me vs. Me. It's the brutal war of comparison, not in the realm of comparing myself to others, but comparing myself to myself. How does one even do that you might ask?

Well, I compare myself to who I used to be. What I used to be. What I used to look like. What I used to be able to do. The best versions of myself compared to the worst versions of myself. Can you see now why I try not to compare myself with other women very often...my hands are completely full comparing my "now" self to my "old" self. I don't have the time or the energy to play that game with other women because I am playing that game with myself just about every day. Remember when I said that no one ever wins this game? Well, try playing this losing game with yourself...it really is lose-lose.

I played softball growing up and loved it. I usually played infield and worked hard at practice to be my best. I played on my High School Varsity team and remember how honored I was to win the Leadership Award my senior year. Then I graduated. Softball wasn't on the schedule anymore. I missed it. When I was nineteen, my friend Jennifer told me about an adult ladies softball league at her church. I signed up and began playing again. I was young, really young and was still pretty good. You know what, I played in that same league for almost 20 more years. The only summers I skipped were the ones when I was pregnant. I would've played even then but I knew I wouldn't be able to make myself NOT slide if the play was close. So, I coached those summers instead. As my softball years continued, I began to see a pattern that I didn't like. I was getting older and the other girls on the teams were getting younger. While they were diving for balls, I was falling over balls. While they were stretching doubles into triples, I was just praying I had stretched. They were pulling the ball down the first base line and I was just pulling muscles. I remember one game where I was flying into the parking lot two minutes before game time. I yanked my two small girls out of the car, handed them to their daddy, and hustled to the first base line to pray with the team. I got there just in time. Just in time to be the first batter and just in time to tear my right quadricep as I hit a ball and burst out of the batter's box. See, I didn't stretch before-hand. Thirty-something muscles need some stretching or they will just go ahead and snap on ya. Nice. I was out several games because of it too. Guess what? Now, every time I look at my right quad, I see the large raised knot where my muscle healed incorrectly. Just great. I can't even heal correctly anymore.

I began to see that my ability on the softball field was waning. I wasn't as good as I used to be. I wasn't as fast as I used to be. I couldn't hit the ball as hard or as far as I used to. There I was, sitting on that hard wooden bench, seeing that the thing I used to be really good at, I was just okay at now. Mediocre at best. I didn't have to compare myself to the other players to know this truth.

All I had to do was hold up what I used to be able to do with what I could do now, and see. See the failure. See the "not good enough". See the comparison. See the loss. Me vs. Me.

When I look at how certain abilities have changed over the years, it's hard. It's hard to see greatness in that ability and as time goes by, that greatness isn't so great anymore. How does one reconcile that? How does someone reconcile the fact that they aren't what they used to be? It feels like a loss...and losing stinks.

Decreasing abilities are only one aspect of this battle for me. My biggest, nastiest, ugliest, hardest battle when it comes to Me vs. Me is physically. What I used to look like compared to what I look like now. My forty-something year old self compared to everything before

> It's hard to see greatness in that ability and as time goes by, that greatness isn't so great anymore.

that. I see pictures of myself from years ago and nothing good happens on the inside of me. I don't think to myself, "Self, you sure did look good in that bikini"! Instead I think to myself, "Self, how could you let yourself look like you do now? You couldn't get in that bikini again if you tried. And even if you could actually get into it, you certainly wouldn't look like THAT! You're kind of gross now." I see the amount of pictures that I allowed to be taken of me years ago compared to the four pictures I've allowed to be taken of me now. It didn't used to matter what angle a picture was taken of me back then. Most every angle was acceptable. Not now. Now, I have to turn my shoulder just right so my arm doesn't look ginormous but, I still need my arm to be able to cover some of my muffin top as well. It's these moments I wish I was an octopus so I could use all eight of those arms to cover something I want to remain hidden or camouflaged. I have to look at the camera a certain way so you can't see my double chin but also tilt my head to the right so my face doesn't look as "full" as it usually does in pictures. "Full" means round. "Round" means fat. Folks could make an Olympic event out of trying to get an acceptable picture of me. It's simply exhausting. Just so you know, when you take a group picture and someone says, "Is it good?" they are really just asking if THEY look good. Just sayin. I keep telling myself that I will regret not having more pictures taken of me with my kids but honestly, I just can't even bare to see myself in print. If I do take a picture with one of my kids, I just hide behind them.

They have no idea that their mom is struggling. Drowning in the sea of comparison. Gasping for breath.

I started working out when my first baby was seven weeks old. I had never worked out before and was so intimidated but a kind friend showed me the way. I fell in love with working out. No, I'm serious, I really did. Stop laughing, I really did love doing it! I wasn't a huge fan of the cardio aspect of it but I LOVED lifting weights. In fact, I always say that I don't run unless I'm chasing a cake. Or cupcakes. Or cookies. And some pies. Anyway, I felt strong and liked feeling that way. After a while, I could see the results and I was so happy. I felt strong and I looked strong. In my twenties and most of my thirties I was strong and fit. Every now and then, an older woman would say to me, "You just wait honey...it gets harder. When you hit forty it won't be the same." Then, she'd turn herself around and saunter away. I would secretly roll my eyes (well, not always so secretly) and let out a dramatic sigh. Not me. It won't happen to me, I would think to myself.

But then it did. Oh how it did. My forties have been hard. Like trying-to-pass-a-calculus-test-you-never-studied-for hard. Like trying-to-thread-a-needle-without-your-glasses kind of hard. Like running-a-marathon-when-you-trained-for-a-5k kind of hard. Are you picking up what I'm throwing down? Hard. My metabolism is different. My eating and cravings are different. My workouts are different. To top it all off I had a hysterectomy at forty-one and couldn't exercise for about eight weeks, which turned into eight months. Imagine what eight weeks...ummm...okay, months, of no workouts and yummy food from very caring people did to my already-struggling body? Ughhhh!

So, I struggle. I battle. I war. Comparison is a cruel, cruel game. Especially when played against yourself. When I get to the bones of it, this type of comparison hinges on two words..."used to". I "used to" look like that. I "used to" be good at that. I "used to" have

> Comparison is a cruel, cruel game. Especially when played against yourself.

that. Used to. Two teeny, tiny words with such a huge impact. Those two words hold an ideal. A standard. When I compare my "now" to my "used to", I'm below standard. I'm sub-par. I don't measure up. It messes with me. It makes me feel "less-than".

I ran across this Scripture just recently and it hit me square between the eyes...hard...just like my forties have been. 2 Corinthians 10:12 "...When they measure themselves by themselves and compare themselves with themselves, they are not wise." Ummmm...ouch. Double ouch. I just got called out! Now, was Paul writing this to me? No, he was actually writing it to the false teachers in Corinth who thought there was no standard of comparison higher than themselves. However, I read it and knew I could learn from it. I want to be wise. This verse tells me that if I measure my "former" self to my "now" self and compare my "used to" self to my "not anymore" self, then I am not wise. I am a fool. I can hear "Mr. T" holler at me now, "I pity the fool!". I don't want "Mr. T" to pity me. Or holler at me. I don't want to be a fool anymore. I don't want to lose anymore. I'm really tired of it.

So, where do I go from here? In no way do I think I will magically be "fixed" from this self-induced battle. But the battle of Me vs. Me has one huge weapon that I wasn't counting on. One word. One amazing word. *GRACE.* Not the kind of grace that saves your soul from hell. We receive that grace when we accept Jesus Christ as our Lord and Savior. This is a different type of grace. It's the kind of grace that says, "It's okay. You're okay." My sister often tells me, "You really need to cut yourself some slack. You are so hard on yourself." I hate it when she's right. This is the kind of grace that I need to battle with in my war on comparison. This type of grace doesn't negate the beauty of what once was, but it also doesn't forgo the beauty of what is now. It's the type of grace that acknowledges the validity of the beauty in the past without robbing someone of the significance of the beauty in the present. I am learning to get to the place that I can see what once was as just that...it once was... and it's okay that it once was. I am no longer in that place in my life good OR bad because I'm here, in the present, and the present is beautiful, even if it is different. Whether it be my abilities or my physical being, I am working on understanding that grace needs to win in this battle of comparison.

Does this mean I shouldn't take care of my body? That I should eat how I really WANT to eat? To skip my workouts and nap instead? Does this grace mean that I shouldn't try to improve on the abilities that I have or give up on the ones that I'm not so good at anymore? Yes. Yes it does. I'm kidding, I just wanted to see if you were actually reading these words or just skipping over them! Obviously that is not what this grace means. I still have to do all of those things. That's my part. But that's only half of it. The other half? Well, it is bestowing grace when and where I need it.

I'm learning this and will not say that I have mastered it in the least. But it's a start. A good start. A grace-full start. Paul says it best in Philippians 3:12-14 "Not that I have already obtained all this, or have already been made perfect, but I press on to take hold of that for which Christ Jesus took hold of me. {Sisters}, I do not consider myself yet to have taken hold of it. But one thing I do: Forgetting what is behind and straining toward what is ahead, I press on toward the goal to win the prize for which God has called me heavenward in Christ Jesus."

Applying grace to myself isn't easy but neither is the battle of Me vs. Me. I just have to choose my hard.

This type of grace doesn't negate the beauty of what once was, but it also doesn't forgo the beauty of what is now. It's the type of grace that acknowledges the validity of the beauty in the past without robbing someone of the significance of the beauty in the present.

Embracing who I am now, my abilities, my appearance, and all that comes with it is a process. A process that will lead to freedom. I believe that, I really do. I recently ran across a quote that said, "I love who I've been, but I really love who I'm becoming." I liked that. I liked it a lot. It seemed to speak grace to both parts of me. The "used to" as well as "who I am now". I do love who I've been. And now I'm able to say that I love who I'm becoming. So now, even though my thighs are bigger, I've come to realize that so is my heart. While I don't normally compare myself to other women, I do compare myself to what I consider to be the best version of me. But I've come to realize that my measuring stick is broken. Very broken. I'm asking God to show me how to do all of this well. And what I know of God is that He will. He always does.

I know this was a hard chapter to read. I know that because it was a hard chapter to write. Thank you for letting me write it. It's messy. I'm messy. This is real life. Isn't it about time we all start doing "real" anyway? None of us have it all together. None of us. Even that woman you think could not possibly struggle with anything, does. We are all fighting this comparison battle in some shape, form, or fashion. Some of us do it quietly, some of us don't. So, I guess in a way, my freedom begins today. I choose grace and it chooses me. In the battle of Me vs. Me, I will let grace win. And win it will.

Me vs. Me
Study Guide

1. What did Karen explain Me vs. Me to mean?

_____

_____

_____

_____

2. Can you relate to any of Karen's struggles?

_____

_____

_____

_____

3. Karen said that this type of comparison hinged on two words. What were they and why are they so impactful?

_____

_____

_____

_____

4. "This type of grace doesn't negate the beauty of what once was, but it also doesn't forgo the beauty of what is now. It's the type of grace that acknowledges the validity of the beauty in the past without robbing someone of the

significance of the beauty in the present."
What does this quote speak to you?

_____

_____

_____

_____

_____

_____

Abba, Father, there is no one greater! I humbly come to you with my doubts and ask for your truth to satisfy my soul. When I question my purpose or why am I not like I used to be, help me remember that You knew me before you formed me. You knit me together in my mother's womb with a specific plan just for me. You are my creator and I am Your masterpiece. You are not finished with me yet. Let me see me through Your eyes. When I feel like I can't do anything right, help me to claim that when I am weak, You alone are strong. Teach me to stay completely dependent on You. I believe that Your ways are so much higher than mine and that You know what is best for me. You are for me!

When I hear the lies of the enemy telling me I am not good enough, that I am not qualified, that I don't "have it" anymore, sing over me. Let me hear Your melody and feel your presence in every fiber of my being. May it soothe my soul. You love me!

When I have no more fight, let me remember that You fight my battles. My job is simply to give it to You and trust. You have gone before me!

When I am broken, I know that I am not alone. You see my scars and they are beautiful. Let me see beauty from the ashes. You are close to the brokenhearted and you save those who are crushed in spirit. You are my comforter!

When I am afraid, I will trust in You, God. I will take my thoughts captive in obedience to You. I will hide in the shadow of Your wings. You are my protector!

When You search, Father, let my heart be found to be completely Yours. I surrender my "used to be" for the "present me" trusting that You have me right where You want me.

Oh, Father, I know that Your masterpiece will be spectacular! Thank You for grace, upon grace, upon grace, upon grace. I am all Yours.

This prayer was written and prayed over you by my wise and loving friend, Crista Andrews.

Mirror, Mirror, on the Wall...

Doesn't that title remind you of a certain black-haired, red cheeked, princess who ate a bad apple? Or, better yet, the narcissistic queen who had an inferiority complex? I don't think I will ever forget the queen staring into her magic mirror and reciting those words, "Mirror, mirror, on the wall, who's the fairest of them all?" The queen was used to having that mirror show her, her own reflection, which would fuel her desire to be the fairest, the best, and the most beautiful. One day, the queen uttered those magic words to that magic mirror and something not-so-very-magical happened. Her reflection was absent. It wasn't her own face staring back at her. Instead, it was the young, beautiful face of Snow White. The magic mirror had declared *her* the "fairest of them all". That sent the queen into a royal tizzy. The queen wasn't so thrilled with the mirror after all.

See, this is where I can relate. I have a love-hate relationship with mirrors. I love to hate them. As much as I loathe them, I sure seem to have a lot of them around. My favorite mirror, if I have to have one, is the mirror in my daughter, Josey's room. I call it the "skinny mirror". See why I like that one so much? I'm not sure why, but that mirror always makes me look like a skinny-minnie! I am acutely aware that it is an inaccurate depiction of reality. Let me translate that for you, "I know it ain't the way I really look!" I also have the mirror that is attached to my dresser. I affectionately call that my "large and in charge" mirror. Mainly because that is the way I appear in it...large...and in charge. I also have my make-up mirror in the bathroom. I have the opportunity to get up-close and personal with that one. Then, there is the mirror I have named the "truth serum" mirror. It is the mirror glued to the back of my sun visor in my car. That thing will tell you more than you want to know sister. I will have just left my make-up mirror thinking my face is all put together and with one glimpse from the "truth serum" mirror, I realize that my foundation is not blended in, my contour looks like a three year old did it with her eyes closed, and I have a precarious hair sticking out of my beauty mark. Okay, I have more than one hair sticking out of that beauty mark but whatever. I feel like I could be in another children's story...The Three Little Pigs: "Little Pig, Little Pig let me in!"

"Not by the hair on Karen's chinnie, chin, chin!"

But let me tell you without a doubt, the absolute WORST mirrors in the history of all the world are located in dressing rooms. Can I get a witness? In fact, I don't even call it a dressing room anymore. I call it, "The Den of Death." I believe that adequately describes one of those places. And let me just ask ya'll this while we're at it, who, in Pete's blazes, ever thought it would be a good idea to place florescent lighting in that Den of Death? I bet it was a man. No woman in her right mind would have ever decided to put that type of lighting in there. Do you know what I call the lighting in those wretched Dens? Cellulighting...that's what. It is a well-known fact that the lighting in those dressing rooms shine light directly onto the areas of our bodies that do not need to be lit up. Ever. Hold me Jesus. Now listen, I know it's humiliating for that light to shine on those dimples strategically placed on the backs of our thighs, but ya'll...have you ever looked AT YOUR FACE in that mirror? I have. Now I need counseling. That mirror can also be called "The Pore Mirror". It sounds like "Poor Mirror" because that's how I feel about my "poor" face. All those "Poor Pores" just showing up all over the place. It's like the moon...on my face...craters and pores galore. Fix it Jesus.

Can you see now why I have such an issue with mirrors? They all say something different. I am not sure which reflection is accurate. Which reflection do I believe, do I trust, do I hold on to? Which mirror is actually revealing the truth about me? How do I see myself? Better yet, how does God see me?

Imagine entering a room and in it you see three, full-length, stand-alone mirrors. Each mirror has a different word boldly written across it. The first mirror has the word "Past" written on it. The second mirror says, "Present", and the third mirror, "Future". Let's take a closer look at these mirrors...but not too close, you may just find one of those stray hairs!

The Mirror of Your Past

As you look into the mirror of your past, what do you see? My guess is you see some words flash across that mirror like: regret, shame, wrong decisions and poor choices. Or how about embarrassment, guilt, failure, and sin? This doesn't mean you don't have some great memories in your past but, that mirror is a reminder of what went wrong. What failed. What messed up. The mirror of your past doesn't bring you joy or peace. It brings you shame and guilt. Let

> Often, when we look in the mirror of our past, we are reminded of all that is unredeemable about us. All that is broken and worthless. We see our past as a series of checks and balances and we are way overdrawn.

me tell you something about shame and guilt, it doesn't look good on anybody. Kind of like wearing leggings as pants, know what I mean?

Often, when we look in the mirror of our past, we are reminded of all that is unredeemable about us. All that is broken and worthless. We see our past as a series of checks and balances and we are way overdrawn. When we stare at our reflection in this mirror, we feel defeated. We wish we could go back, start over, fix it all. But we can't and we know we can't, which just makes it even worse.

Have you ever considered what God may see when He looks at your past? It feels awkward and uncomfortable to think of God looking at our past doesn't it? He sees it alright. But what exactly does He see? I'll give you two words...His Son. He sees His Son Jesus. 2 Corinthians 5:21 says, "God made him who had no sin to be sin for us, so that in him we might become the righteousness of God." The Message says it like this, "God put the wrong on him who never did anything wrong, so we could be put right with God." He doesn't see the list of wrongs, the sins, the mess-ups, and the failures that came with those words that flashed across that mirror we mentioned earlier. He doesn't see the thing that you are most ashamed about and he certainly doesn't see a guilty verdict hanging over your head. He sees His perfect, blameless, and holy Son, stretched out on a bloodied cross. Your forgiveness rests on Jesus, and Jesus is the only thing God sees.

It's humbling isn't it? The fact that your past is messy and ugly and full of guilt but you didn't have to suffer the consequences, Jesus did. He went to the cross so you wouldn't have to. John 3:16 "This is how much God loved the world: He gave his Son, his one and only Son. And this is why: so that no one need be destroyed; by believing in him, anyone can have a whole and lasting life." The Message. Because God chose to make this beautiful sacrifice on your behalf, when He looks at the mirror of your past, He only sees the perfection of His Son.

It's important for me to share that God can only look at the mirror of your past and see His Son if, and only if, you have chosen to say "yes" to a relationship with God, through Christ. If you have never made that decision, then you must know that when God looks at the mirror of your past, He sees hell. That is the cost of sin without Jesus covering it with His blood. Hell is not a theory, it is a real place where real people go when they don't choose salvation. How can you say yes to a relationship with God through His Son and know that God will see your past through Jesus? Romans 10:9 says, "If you declare with your mouth, "Jesus is

> It's important for me to share that God can only look at the mirror of your past and see His Son if, and only if, you have chosen to say "yes" to a relationship with God, through Christ.

Lord," and believe in your heart that God raised him from the dead, you will be saved." You can declare it with your mouth by praying this prayer in the quietness of your heart, "Dear God, I believe that you sent Jesus to die on the cross for me because I am a sinner. I believe that You raised Him from the dead on the third day. I'm asking you to forgive me for all my sins and I'm asking you to save me. I give you my heart and my life. Thank you for saving me in Jesus Name Amen." Oh girl, if you decided to make that your prayer, then welcome to the family sister!

Some of you struggle with the mirror of your past not because of how God sees it, but because of how **you** see it. You can't shake it. You can't gloss over it. You can't forgive it and you certainly can't forget it. How, in the world, are you supposed to **not** think about all of the stuff in that mirror? It's like baggage that you drag behind you everywhere you go. You know the kind of baggage, the kind that has the handle and the wheels. It's a pain to cart it everywhere you go but you don't really know what else to do with it. So, you drag it, roll it, weave it in and out of places. You bump into it. It rolls over your toes. It makes you tired, and frustrated, and sad. This, my baggage-lugging-friend, is what Isaiah 5:18 is talking about; "What sorrow for those who drag their sins behind them with ropes made of lies, who drag wickedness behind them like a cart!" (NLT) What sorrow indeed! The ropes you are holding on to are made of lies, pure lies. The baggage you are dragging behind you brings you sorrow but you keep holding on to that rope, dragging and carting the past around. So, how are you supposed to just "forget" all of the things you are the most ashamed about? How do you stop worrying about what you've done? First, drop the rope. Yep, drop it like it's hot. After you drop the rope of lies that is attached to your baggage, do what Isaiah 43:18 says; "Forget the former things; do not dwell on the past." Why should you forget? Because God does, that's why! "For I will forgive their wickedness and will remember their sins no more." Hebrews 8:12. I remember hearing a radio preacher talk about how God forgets our sins. I loved his

> The ropes you are holding on to are made of lies, pure lies. The baggage you are dragging behind you brings you sorrow but you keep holding on to that rope, dragging and carting the past around.

perspective on it. He said that God doesn't "forget" our sins because He's forgetful or because He has long-term memory loss or even because He just can't remember our sins. It's because He chooses not to. He CHOOSES not to remember our sins any more. He made a choice to not remember. It's His choice and you have to make it yours too. Drop the rope and forget about it.

I think we would all agree that some of those things in our past should not be repeated, correct? I have a hair-style or two that I would like to file under,

> We are supposed to learn from our past, not live there.

"someone should have told me not to" or "what was I thinking?" But I think that is where we get hung up. We are supposed to learn from our past, not live there. Rick Warren says, "We are products of our past, but we don't have to be prisoners of it." Our past has **shaped** us, no doubt, but it does not **have to** define us. Speaking of mirrors, have you ever wondered why the rear-view mirror in a car is so much smaller than the windshield? The rear-view is for looking at what has passed. The windshield is for looking at what is ahead. We don't need to be constantly looking behind us, we're not going that way.

Remember that full-length, stand-alone mirror? The one with the word "Past" on it? Look at it

> Our past has **shaped** us, no doubt, but it does not **have to** define us

again. Now what do you see? My hope is that you will see the same beautiful picture that God, Himself, sees. *His Son*. That's one thing you will never have to forget.

The Mirror of your Present

When you look in the mirror, what do you see? Honestly? Well, most of us would probably say that we see what's wrong with us. What isn't perfect. What isn't pleasant. The blemishes and the spots. The bumps and rolls. The wrinkles and the greys. It's hard for us to look in the mirror and think, "Wow...beautiful!" It's hard for us to see it. It's even harder for us to believe it.

What about God? What do you think He sees when He looks at the mirror of your present?

*God sees beauty.

Don't you roll your eyes at me. He really does see beauty! How can He see ALL of us as beautiful you might ask? Well, that's a good question. I've seen myself in the morning and I'm pretty sure I wouldn't qualify! Genesis 1:27 tells us that we were created in His image...in God's image and isn't He beautiful? Have you ever seen God? I would say probably not. But, doesn't your spirit, your soul, your guts, just know He is beautiful? I may have never SEEN God, but his beauty is displayed everywhere. The splendor of the mountains. The sights and the sounds of the ocean. Trees, flowers, sunrises, sunsets, rainbows, and even rain. Have you ever held a newborn baby? Aren't they beautiful? Yes, I know they are kind of gross when they're born with all that cheesy stuff on them but when you look at that baby, when you behold that tiny creation, don't you see God? Don't you see His handiwork? All of the things I've mentioned are just the overflow from a beautiful Creator. He is beautiful and the

> So how can every single woman on the face of the earth be considered beautiful? Because God is the one defining beauty, not man.

things He creates are beautiful. God is beautiful and you were created in His likeness which means that you, beloved, are beautiful too.

In a world where we are constantly being told who is beautiful and what constitutes beauty, this is a very difficult truth to grasp. We all look so different. Our hair color, our skin color, our eye color, the shape of our bodies, how tall we are, how much we weigh, all of those things are uniquely individual. So how can every single woman on the face of the earth be considered beautiful? Because God is the one defining beauty, not man. When man does it, he describes the outward display of loveliness, but not God.

1 Samuel 16:7 says, "The Lord does not look at the things man looks at. Man looks at the outward appearance, but the

> See, beauty isn't what is ON us, it's what He sees IN us.

LORD looks at the heart." See, beauty isn't what is ON us, it's what He sees IN us. John Eldredge wrote the book, Captivating: Unveiling the Mystery of a Women's Soul, and in it he says, "Because she bears the image of God. She doesn't have to conjure it, go get it from a salon, or have plastic surgery. No, beauty is an essence that is given to every woman at her creation." Shut the front door ya'll. Did you GET that? Beauty is *given* to every woman. Every.Single.Woman. God is the One doing the giving and He doesn't give sparingly. Don't you just love it? Don't you feel beautiful? You should, because you were created in the image of God and He's the most beautiful thing that has ever been.

*God sees worth.

Maybe you've been told that you are worthless. That you will never amount to anything. Maybe you've been told by other people's actions that you hold no value. Maybe it used to be something that you had *heard* about yourself, but now it's something you *believe* about yourself. That belief has now settled into your soul. It has dug deep roots and refuses to let go. Because you feel like you have no value or worth, you have allowed people to treat you as such. You have settled for less. You've accepted less. You've treated yourself as less.

God sees you differently, beloved. So very differently. Do you remember earlier when I shared with you that God sent His only Son to die on a cross for you? Well, let me camp out there for a second. Remember John 3:16, "For God so loved the world, that he gave his only

Son, that whoever believes in him should not perish but have eternal life."? Look at that little two letter word near the beginning. The word "so". Do you see it? Okay. Now read it like this, "For God SO loved the world, that he gave his only Son, that whoever believes in him should not perish but have eternal life." SO. He SO loved you. He SO loved me. God doesn't just love you a little. He loves you SO much that He chose to sacrifice His only Son in your place. If you are a mama, could you grasp the thought of allowing your child to die in someone else's place? Someone you don't know or worse yet, someone who you do know but isn't a very good person? I wouldn't. I couldn't. But God did. That shows you just how much worth you hold in His eyes. He values you and you, my friend, have worth to Him. SO much worth. Your value to Him is equal to that of the life and death of His precious Son

> Your value to Him is equal to that of the life and death of His precious Son.

Have you ever had a pet bird? A canary maybe? I don't know a lot about birds especially because I always had their adversaries as pets. The Cat. My childhood cat, Tigger, was an avid bird hunter. That's probably not a completely accurate statement. He didn't necessarily just hunt birds, he ate them. And what he didn't eat, he left at my doorstep for me to see and celebrate. That was sweet of him wasn't it? Poor bird. I always felt bad for Tigger's latest conquest. Do you know who else knew about Tigger's victim? The Lord. Hard to believe isn't it? It's hard to believe that the Lord of all creation, the God of the universe would concern Himself with my cat's dinner, but He did. Luke 12:6-7 says, "Are not five sparrows sold for two copper coins? Yet not one of them has ever been forgotten in the presence of God. Indeed the very hairs of your head are all numbered. Do not be afraid; you are far more valuable than many sparrows." God knows the condition of every sparrow, every canary, every meal fallen at the claws of my cat. They matter to Him. They are His

> When God looks at you, He sees worth and He sees value. Years of hearing differently tend to cloud this truth but I am here to tell you that God deems you worthy. Worthy of His Son, worthy of His love, worthy of His attention.

creation. If God knows the condition of every bird, and they're just birds, imagine what He thinks about you! When God looks at you, He sees worth and He sees value. Years of hearing differently tend to cloud this truth but I am here to tell you that God deems you worthy. Worthy of His Son, worthy of His love, worthy of His attention. I can only imagine how difficult it must be to shift your thinking from years of feeling that you have no worth to someone telling you that you have the ultimate worth. Take a breath and read this section again and again until you begin to grasp the idea that you do have value and worth. Great worth. Worth far beyond your ability to understand. God sees it. God believes it. He wants you to see it and believe it too.

*God sees purpose.

When you look at your life, do you see purpose? God does. He looks at the mirror of your present and He sees a clear cut purpose for you, even if you don't. Rick Warren, the author of The Purpose Driven Life says, "If you're alive, there's a purpose for your life." God has the same outlook. Ephesians 2:10 NLT, "For we are God's masterpiece. He has created us anew in Christ Jesus, so we can do the good things he planned for us long ago."

We weren't created to just exist. We were created for a purpose, a purpose and a plan greater than ourselves and God knows it. I wish I could tell you your specific purpose but I can't. Just know that God sees that purpose when He looks at you. You're important. You matter. You matter to this world and you matter to His Kingdom. As believers, we all have one unified purpose and it is found in the New Testament. Mark 16:15 lays it out for us, "And He said to them, "Go into all the world and preach the gospel to all creation." I know what you are thinking, "Whoooaaa...wait a minute little Miss Thang, I'm no preacher!" Maybe you are, maybe you aren't, but this verse is not speaking to your career choice, it is speaking to how you make much of the Name of Jesus IN your career choice as well as your life. It's the idea of taking whatever it is that is deep within you and sharing it with others so that God is magnified. Our main purpose is to share the gospel of Jesus Christ. How we do that will align with the giftings He's set in our hearts.

Have you ever met someone who truly shines and radiates the love and the mission of the Lord? Like everything they do is wrapped in this special favor of God and everything they touch, speak about, or look upon just shines with Jesus? I have and it's beautiful. Do you know what I've learned about people like that? I've learned that they became His light when they understood what their specific purpose was for Christ. They honed in on their passion and began walking it out in such a way that the gospel is preached, sometimes without ever even saying a word. When a person seeks to find their specific purpose, they have done a great thing. "The purposes of a person's heart are deep waters, but one who has insight draws them out." Proverbs 20:5 A wise person knows the importance of seeking what they were created for. I love that Lysa Terkeurst explains it as "your soul thing". Your soul thing is that thing that stirs you, the passion that pushes you, the fire that ignites you. This is how we preach. By using the giftings God has given us for His glory and to point right to the very God we serve and celebrate! Your purpose is unique and important, just like you! You matter so much in this world, and to Him, that it's said there's something you can do better than 10,000 other people. So, find out what it is, do it, and do it often. When God

> Your soul thing is that thing that stirs you, the passion that pushes you, the fire that ignites you. This is how we preach.

looks at you, He sees your purpose and He desires for you to see it too.

The Mirror of your Future

When you look at your future what do you see? Success or struggle? Freedom or fear? Focus or frustration? What thoughts come to your mind when you think of your tomorrow? I'm sure we'd all love a crystal ball every now and then just to see what was ahead. To see what was around the corner, waiting for us. A better job, a happy family, fabulous friends, a beautiful new car, and a great church home. Or are we afraid that no good thing awaits? A terrible job, a divorce, no friends, a broken car, and no church family. When you look in the mirror of your future, are you excited about the opportunities or dreading the options? Have you ever wondered about what God sees when He looks at your future? Well, truth be told, He sees every specific part of your future but when it comes to you and your tomorrow, what does He see? Jeremiah 29:11 The Message says, "I know what I'm doing, I have it all planned out – plans to take care of you, not abandon you, plans to give you the future you hope for." Wow, that doesn't sound so daunting, or scary, or terrible does it? When God looks at you in light of your tomorrow, He sees some amazing things.

*God sees potential

When God looks in the mirror of your future, He doesn't need a crystal ball because He sees it all. All of it, including your potential. Potential is defined as latent qualities or abilities that may be developed and lead to future success or usefulness. The definition of latent is existing, but not yet developed, hidden or concealed. So, God sees existing, but not yet developed qualities and abilities in you that will lead to success or usefulness. It's what we call "untapped potential". Potential is hard because it's not something that is easy for us to see. Potential has to do with what "will be" and

> Potential is hard because it's not something that is easy for us to see. Potential has to do with what "will be" and we are always so consumed with "what is".

we are always so consumed with "what is".

What potential could God possibly see in you? The potential to change the world. Does that sound too lofty for you? Okay. How about the potential to change a continent? Still too big? Well, how about the potential to change your country, your state, your town? Are those still kind of mind blowing to you? I understand. So, let me bring this home for you on a closer level. God sees in you the potential to make an impact on your family. The kind of impact that will last for all of eternity. To raise children to be lovers of Jesus and to teach their children to do the same. God sees in you the ability to be a catalyst for raising world-changers. The ones who will chase down hunger on mission trips. The ones who will break laws by smuggling Bibles to places that don't allow it. The ones who stand for Christ regardless of the consequences and the ones who show His love to every single person placed in front of them no matter their race, their beliefs, or their ideologies. You may be the very person to raise the person who finds a cure for cancer. It might be your DNA who discovers a way to stop hunger. The next Billy Graham could be born and cradled by you. You have the ability to invest in your family to such a degree that they become the change in the world we all long to see. This doesn't just mean your children, you know. This same potential to make a lasting impact can be used to encourage your husband as well. Speak life, promise, encouragement, and power into him as he goes into his world. "Treat people as if they were what they should be and you help them become what they are capable of becoming." Johann Wolfgang von Goethe. You have the potential to hand him a sword to go slay his dragons. Sounds powerful doesn't it? Well, you also have the potential to hand him a toothpick. That speaks to the lack of belief that you have in him to do what he was made to do. Your potential to make an impact in your husband's life can be as powerful as handing him what you think he can handle in his fight, a sword or a toothpick. Both of them speak to the confidence you have in him. One speaks more loudly than the other.

God sees potential not only in your ability to impact your family, but those you work with as well. You have the ability to change the atmosphere at your workplace. I bet you just laughed and laughed at that last statement because you think I don't know the environment in which you work. You're right, I don't, but God does. He wants to use you in the place that you show up to at least five days a week, to make a forever impact for His Kingdom. He recognizes the ability that you have to love, to serve, to show kindness, to encourage, to pray with and to pray for those who are there. He sees the untapped potential in your ability to make a difference for Jesus in the workplace. Yes, she may be impossible to be around. And yes, he may be annoying. They may be ungrateful. She may throw you under the bus to your bosses. He may criticize every little thing you do. But, what if God has you there just for those people? What if He has placed you in the middle of mayhem in order to make much of the Name of Jesus. To point to Him in all things. To show that you don't serve man, you serve God, but in serving God you also will be willing to serve man as well. To love with no expectations. To give without strings. To help with pure motives. God sees that in you, the potential exists to do more. To be a game changer. A work changer. A world changer. When He looks into the mirror of your future, He sees the potential you have to make an impact on whatever circle He has placed you in. A forever impact, a powerful impact, a lasting impact. I am praying that it will be untapped no longer.

God can look at you today and see the potential for tomorrow. My prayer for you is that of the apostle Paul as he wrote to the church at Ephesus, "I pray also that the eyes of your heart may be enlightened in order that you may know the hope to which he has called you, the riches of his glorious inheritance in the saints…"

Ephesians 1:18 I pray that the eyes of your heart may see because maybe your natural eyes can't. You have such great potential to impact others for your King.

*God sees Growth

When the Lord looks at the mirror of your future, He sees someone who is growing, maturing, reaching important milestones. Your future self won't be in the same place that you are today and that's how it should be! Philipians 1:6 says, "...being confident of this, that he who began a good work in you will carry it on to completion until the day of Christ Jesus." This verse denotes growth. Yes, there's a beginning and an end. But don't miss the in-between. The growth. The forward motion. The movement from one place to another.

God sees you growing in all aspects of your life and one of those ways

> You don't serve man, you serve God, but in serving God you also will be willing to serve man as well. To love with no expectations. To give without strings. To help with pure motives.

is spiritually. 2 Peter 3:18 says, "…but grow in the grace and knowledge of our Lord and Savior Jesus Christ. To Him be the glory, both now and to the day of eternity. Amen." God sees you growing in Him. In His ways, in His knowledge, in His love, and in His grace.

He sees you doing the things in your future that will allow growth to happen in the spiritual realm. Staying connected to your local church and being in a body of believers is imperative. I believe in the body of Christ and what it can bring to a person's life. Personally, I've experienced the most growth when I committed to joining small groups at church. There is just something dynamic that happens when you put people together who are walking similar journeys at similar times. Doing life together promotes growth, deep growth in fact, so be ready to join a small group and experience exponential growth!

Reading the Bible is another way that you will experience growth. This tends to be quite intimidating to most people so they avoid it. Maybe it does the same for you. Let me take a load off, you don't have to read the whole Bible, unless you just want to! There are devotionals out there that have one Scripture to chew on at a time so it's not so overwhelming. Some people read a chapter a day, some read more than that. Whatever will keep you linked to the One you are following. When you read the Bible, you are reading God's heart for you. His Word teaches you how to live this life. It gives wisdom, and clarity, and direction to your spirit. Whether you take the time to read a devotional, a verse, or a chapter, you will grow and your spirit will soar!

Another way that helps me grow spiritually is listening to worship music. Some may wonder how that helps a person grow because it's just music but it does something to me. It moves me. It moves me forward in my relationship with my King. The worship songs remind me of what He's done, what He is currently doing, and what He will do in me and that makes me draw near to Him. Every time you draw near to Him, you grow.

> Every time you draw near to Him, you grow.

I can tell you what was happening in my life at certain times based on the worship song that I hear. The music, the words, the worship, all take me to a place where I grow in Him. So, the next time you are in the car, you have my permission to turn that worship song up loud, raise your hand (just one, remember you are driving) and grow, grow, grow!

Remember that room? The one with the three mirrors in it? The past, the present, and the future all represented. You don't have to wonder which reflection to believe; believe the truth. Believe what God sees when He gazes into those mirrors. He sees more than you could ever hope for...and that is beautiful...just like you.

> You don't have to wonder which reflection to believe; believe the truth. Believe what God sees when He gazes into those mirrors.

Mirror, Mirror, on the Wall...
Study Guide

1. What does God see when He looks in the mirror of your past? How does that change your own outlook on your past?

_____

_____

_____

_____

2. When God looks in the mirror of your present, He sees:

* _____

* _____

* _____

Which one of these spoke to you and why?

_____

_____

_____

_____

3. When God looks in the mirror of your future, He sees:

* _____

* _____

4. What are some ways you see potential in your future? What are some ways you can grow in the Lord?

_____

_____

_____

_____

_____

Dear Heavenly Father,

I come before you with everything exposed. I have looked at the mirrors of my past, present and future with regrets and fear. You know every night I could not sleep and the mornings I awoke to the condemning voices in my mind. I confess these sins and ask for forgiveness. This day I see and declare the truth of Your Word and it has penetrated my heart. This day I choose to believe the absoluteness, the totality, the completeness of forgiveness given on my behalf through the sacrifice of Your son, Jesus. I acknowledge and accept that you have redeemed and cleansed me with the blood of Christ. This day I claim your promise, therefore, there is now no condemnation for me through Christ Jesus. Lord I ask that you would bring this day, this moment to my memory every time Satan tries to bring doubts and more lies of guilt and shame to my mind. I am so thankful to release this baggage. Keep my mind focused on what you have ahead for me and not on that which is behind me. I praise you Father for evidence of growth in my spiritual life as You continue to open my heart and mind to truth. Help me to continue to seek you in every situation. I know you have only good plans for my future and I trust you completely. I believe you are doing a new thing in me. Thank you for clearing my vision and for genuine excitement for the future. Keep me in the Word, I know this is the only mirror I need. Lord I am so thankful, amazed and humbled by your extreme love. Love like no other. Chosen as yours. In Jesus precious Holy name. Amen

This prayer was written and prayed over you by my humble and amazing aunt, Trish Pearce.

Perfectly Imperfect
Written by Guest Author, Michele Fort

That hat just wouldn't stay on her head. She
needed that hat. That shimmery pink and gold, pointy
princess cone hat with the cascading trail of pink netting
matched the princess dress. And perfectly, I might add.
And that princess dress matched the main character in
her princess book-- perfectly I might add, too. The book
had been our inspiration for her very first character day
at school, where she would march in her very first
parade. We marked and measured the elastic straps on
each side of the hat and sewed one side up, making our
first adjustment. But again, that hat went catawampus,
teetered to one side and slid right off her head. We sewed
the other side up and surprisingly, it held secure. Secure

enough the morning of the parade when I took a few Facebook-worthy pics of her at home, secure enough riding to school and through the carpool line in her car seat and secure enough walking solo inside the building and into her classroom.

An hour later, we all stood in the school parking lot waiting for the parade to begin. The music started, the director made the class introductions and the children holding the welcome banner began to march. It was go time. My mama-searching eyes roamed right and left, scanning cherub faces and colorful costumes, finally resting on my three-year- old daughter. She was following her teacher, holding her book, waving to the onlookers, but minus that hat on her head. In fact, that now infamous hat was dangling from her tiny neck, the fragile fabric crawling on the concrete behind her. What does any good mama do? Well, I'll give you one good guess as to what this good mama did. I had to protect my daughter's premiere princess moment, that's what. The only sensible and loyal thing to do was circle the parade route, wave her down and assist her in getting that hat back in its rightful position. But wouldn't you know it? Five steps back in line and that blasted…I mean, blessed hat fell right back off her head. One more run back to mama, one more attempt to fix it and one more wave from us as our girl followed her class into the building, hat in the exact location it was in when this delightful experience began just ten minutes prior.

Inside at the fall party, we discovered a bow had fallen off her glittery princess shoes. Then, running to greet me, she tripped on the ruffle trim at the bottom of her princess dress and slid her princess self across the tile, head-first. All I could do was scoop my damsel in distress up, lean my head back and laugh and relish the joy of holding my daughter in my arms. Our perfect princess ensemble with all its perfect princess preparations had come undone. Perfectly imperfect. That's what we'll call it.

Lesson #1: Hone in on the imperfections less. Pack up those critical eyes and pull out the comical ones. You'll see more clearly, and the view just may make you smile.

Before we venture any farther together, I feel an introduction is in order. My name is Michele. I am a grateful believer in Jesus Christ. I struggle, but am still finding victory, in overcoming perfectionism and some of the symptoms of it: critical eyes, inadequacy, unfair comparisons, being comfortable when my world gets uncomfortable, striving, anger, expectations,

Lesson #1: Hone in on the imperfections less. Pack up those critical eyes and pull out the comical ones. You'll see more clearly, and the view just may make you smile.

disappointment and fear of failure.

This is the type of introduction you may hear if you've ever been invited to a Celebrate Recovery or an AA meeting.

Similar were the words I heard sitting in attendance at my sweet friend's ten-year sobriety anniversary. Ten years of victory over defeat, ten years since my friend became undone. The words my friend shared and the others' testimonials celebrating in attendance with her resonated deeply within me, awakening me to the weight of struggle. One by one, brave souls stood, and took ownership of their choices, their addictions, the consequences, their past and their present. The first bold act in this environment of brutal honesty was represented by walking to the front of the room and taking a chip, the chip of surrender. Standing before the God who created them and friends surrounding them, they admit to the fact they are helpless to fight this battle alone. They willingly choose to become undone. A new posture of humility replaces the stubborn one of sheer will and independence. They come to the realization that on their own, they're not enough. They understand Ann Voskamp's words, "You clearly not being enough is what makes the enoughness of God most clearly seen."

Whenever conflict arises within myself and I see my own desires wavering between wanting things to be just right or feeling like I can't keep my mess together, admission is the first and appropriate response. Especially if I want to get well. This is the point where healing begins. In John 5, Jesus sees a thirty-eight- year-old man who had spent his entire life as an invalid, lying by a pool in Jerusalem. This pool was unique in the sense that a great number of people with

disabilities would lie next to the pool in hopes of getting in at just the right time, the exact moment the water was stirred by an angel of the Lord. Whoever entered the water first would be cured of whatever disease ailed him. Jesus approaches the man, knowing the exact number of hopeless days he'd been lying there and asks, "Do you want to get well?" or "Do you want to be healed?" The man responds saying he has no one to help him into the pool when the water is stirred, and

that some other needy individual always beats him there. Getting to the water took a great deal of hard work. Seemingly ignoring the excuses, Jesus simply commands the man to get up, pick up his mat and walk. With hope-filled faith, the man did just that and was miraculously healed.

One of the hardest things for anyone leaning toward perfectionistic tendencies is an interruption to their normal, comfortable, settled lives. I know this first-hand. Seven years ago, God began stirring the waters of my husband's heart and mine. He began opening our eyes to a need-filled world outside of our own personal family bubble. Through a series of specific, unusual and often unexplainable events over the course of several months, it was clear God was inviting us to follow Him into the waters of international adoption. His beckoning led us to pursue a little girl on another continent, on the other side of the world. We had no idea how long this pursuit would take, what it would look like and how unbearably hard the journey to get her would be, but He told us to, so we did.

> One of the hardest things for anyone leaning toward perfectionistic tendencies is an interruption to their normal, comfortable, settled lives.

Stepping off our mat of comfort, we stepped forward with blind, knee-shaking faith and put our "yes" on the table to follow wherever He led.

Nearly five years later, it was go time. We boarded an airplane for an international flight which carried us across the globe to India. After spending two weeks overseas, we hopped back on a plane, carrying us and our third and youngest daughter (that precious preschooler I may have mentioned at the beginning of this chapter) home. There were times when anxiety nearly engulfed me and when fear almost paralyzed me. I wanted to do it right-- the whole process of waiting well and praying without ceasing as we prepared for her to join our family. I tried really, really hard. But sometimes my desire and my discipline didn't match up. Sometimes I wasn't sure I really wanted what I knew God wanted for us. Our little life, prior to this stirring, seemed perfect. God had already gifted us with two beautiful, intelligent, delightful daughters. We thought our family was whole and complete and that we could actually keep it that way. Silly us! As His children, under His authority, He held the reigns, and continues to do so, concerning the dynamics of our family. On my most conflicted days when I wrestled with not feeling loving enough or patient enough or educated enough about abandonment or trauma wounds, I would lament to God. I told Him my spirit was willing; my flesh was weak. I joined the Psalmist and prayed, "Grant me a willing spirit to sustain me." Confessing my need for Him, my dependence on Him and my struggles gave way to breakthrough after breakthrough. I didn't have to act like I had it all together. I clearly didn't. I was undone. I still am.

At the time I am writing this, much has happened. Our precious one has been home with us and in her forever family for nearly two years. Y'all…I just can't even begin to describe the surprising joy she has brought into our family. Energy and enthusiasm, she has in abundance. She's a seeker of information, asking (so very many) questions and needing (so very many) answers. Music is her jam and books are her delight. For this excitable extrovert, being at church, school or a loved one's home is equivalent to being at a party. When I once thought our family was complete, she was incomplete. She needed a family; she got us, and we got her. Perfectly imperfect us.

Lesson #2: Be honest about what you want. Welcome change? Okay being stirred? Live palms up. God will show up. And own your stuff. That's the only way to be healed.

On our daughter's very first "homeiversary", we wanted to do something special as a family to celebrate. "Homeiversary" is a word I coined for the day we carried her out of the orphanage and into our lives. Maybe you've heard this day referred to as, "Forever Family Day" or "Gotcha Day". Whatever the descriptive, this day often fares as equal in recognition to a birthday concerning those touched by adoption. Since our two older daughters did not make the trip to India with us to get their sister, we wanted to take them somewhere they could experience a taste of India on this special day. Located just an hour from our home is a Hindu temple. And not just an ordinary temple, but one of great beauty and brilliant craftsmanship. Its architecture gave us some semblance of many of the native buildings my husband and I saw while in country. On the same grounds of this temple are fountains, tranquil pools of water, a gift store and an Indian

> Lesson #2: Be honest about what you want. Welcome change? Okay being stirred? Live palms up. God will show up. And own your stuff. That's the only way to be healed.

restaurant. As the temple was open to the public, we all agreed this would be the perfect

way to commemorate this life-changing day in all our lives. We planned to tour the grounds, shop, take pictures and even eat some traditional Indian fare. What I didn't expect was the impact being inside the temple would have on me. The rules for going inside were simple: No shoes. No photography. No cell phones. Respect their place of worship. My head knew that India is often referred to as the "land of a million gods", but my heart wasn't prepared for what we observed. Shrine after shrine built for, and around, statue after statue. In the largest room, a man knelt with hands raised in worship to an elaborately gold-covered one in front of him. A woman, bowing down repeatedly, face to the floor, giving adoration to a completely different ornately jeweled one. My girls stared. I stared. And a silent tear escaped my eye and slid down my face.

Turning the corner and up the stairs, we stumbled upon another room. This one was different, unlike the previous room we'd just left. In the middle of this expansive room, on a platform, stood one, solitary statue. The small statue was roped off and in front of it was a small fountain. Around the perimeter of the room were numerous paintings of this same statue. Each painting described one aspect of this god's story and why he was so revered. We circled the room, reading the panels underneath the painting. But I couldn't concentrate. I couldn't focus. My attention was fixed on the white-clad priest walking in repetitive circles around the statue and his shrine behind me. I watched him for a while, feeling his energy as he passed by me. Was he trying to get in his 10,000 fitness steps for the day? Was he protecting his god from us visitors? Was this part of a ceremony we'd just happened upon?

Curiosity finally got the better of me. I leaned over the rope separating me from him and waved him down. He stopped. I asked if I could ask him a question. Unbothered by my interruption, he kindly said I could. I had to know his "why?" Why was he walking around and around and around? His simple explanation slayed me. He makes these repetitive circles, some days 500 times a day, so that his god will be with him. The sight of his striving, him never feeling certain, never having complete assurance of God's presence with him left me undone. And an unexpected ambush of tears followed. I lost all self-control and composure. Exiting the temple rather hurriedly, we gathered our shoes and found benches outside in the warm spring sunshine, allowing me a moment to gather my emotions. Yet again, God had broken my heart for what breaks His.

That man didn't know. He didn't know Emmanuel, God with us, the one true God who, according the scripture, goes before us, stands by our side and stood in our place. The One who promises He comes to dwell inside us and will never leave us, nor forsake us. That man, worshipping in his temple, trying to honor his god, didn't know. He didn't know the Truth I know. He didn't know the Truth we are teaching our daughters. His idols, made by human hands, hold no innate power, no eternal presence and no comforting peace. The stories told about them promise fulfillment, but will never deliver. Psalm 115:3-7 – "Our God is in the heavens; He does all that He pleases. Their idols are silver and gold, the work of human hands. They have mouths, but do not speak; eyes, but do not see. They have ears, but do not hear; noses, but do not smell. They have hands, but do not feel; feet, but do not walk; and they do not make a sound in their

> He didn't know Emmanuel, God with us, the one true God who, according the scripture, goes before us, stands by our side and stood in our place.

throat."

In this coming undone, my own personal idol worship was illuminated. Years of empty striving. My own 500 worthless steps. My own desire for things to be just right, my perfectionistic tendencies. I saw a lifetime of my own pursuits: performance-based works, achievement, for self-worth or for recognition. All good things. But as my pastor says, "idols when they become ultimate things". In feeling the weight of sorrow for what this man didn't know, I felt the weight of my sin for what I did know. Woe is me! I am undone. For I am a woman of unclean lips and actions. My eyes have seen the King, the LORD of hosts! (Isaiah 6:5, my paraphrase)

> Lesson #3: To all of perfection there is a limit. God found perfection in His Son and doesn't expect it in, or from, us. Striving for wholeness or completeness apart from Jesus is fruitless idolatry. Stop circling your idol and rest. Rest that He is with you and loves you. Perfectly,
>
> imperfect you.

Lesson #3: To all of perfection there is a limit. God found perfection in His Son and doesn't expect it in, or from, us. Striving for wholeness or completeness apart from Jesus is fruitless idolatry. Stop circling your idol and rest. Rest that He is with you and loves you. Perfectly, imperfect you.

My husband and I make a great team. And we have certain things we just do that makes that statement a fact. For example, I am kind-of known around these parts as the idea generator. I am the one in our pair who thinks up fun things to do, places to go, people to see, purchases to make and changes to our home. He helps make them happen. That's not to say that he doesn't have amazing ideas from time to time, or that I don't get my hands dirty in the process, but generally speaking, this is how it's worked with us for the last twenty years of our marriage.

Sometime last year, following a pleasant dinner at home with my people, one of us began a trip down memory lane. I cannot recall exactly who or even what led us in that direction, but nevertheless, all of us wound up on that path (minus the wee one, who was oblivious to the topic of conversation at hand and who was probably still fighting to finish her food before we would let her down to play). The remaining four of us landed eight years in the past, when my teenager was in kindergarten and my middle daughter was just out of diapers. The conversation began happily with my oldest sharing some of her memories from her first real experience with school. I piped up with my fondest memory, the one in which her teacher gave the class an end of the year project. Each student was instructed to write a book report and creatively present it to the class. She even sent home a rubric of what was expected. This former school teacher, now parenting a child in school for the first time ever, jumped at the chance to complete, um…be a part of helping with this assignment.

To read and report, my sweet girl chose a classic princess fairy tale. Think lonely lass with long locks, trapped in a tall tower by a selfish, scheming witch. Yep. That one. After spending the morning guiding my six-year- old as she painstakingly wrote her summary on her perfectly dot and line paper, I drove to the local supercenter and came home with yellow yarn. I measured and cut the yarn. Then I measured and cut some more. I counted and braided and counted and braided. Finally, I rubber-banded all the yarn together, attached it a hairclip and figured out a way to make it secure in my daughter's hair. Now, I know what you must be thinking. Why didn't I just purchase a hairpiece?

First of all, too easy and too generic. Second of all, we are talking pre-Disney flick here. So, no movie equals no costumes equals no wigs in local stores. And for the record, this is also pre-Pinterest, so bonus points for me if you're keeping score.

After the hair issue was settled, I came up with another brilliant idea for how my girl could present her report to the class. Picture this: tall, castle turret with a window cut out in which my sweet girl would peek her head out, let down her fine hair and read her report. Go ahead and add a few more points. I'll wait.

Off I went the next day to meet a friend who allowed me access into a warehouse where I exited with a giant, rectangular piece of thick, white Styrofoam. A couple of cans of castle-silver spray paint and I headed home, anxious to relay all my well-thought out concepts to my kind and helpful husband when he got home from work. An artist I am not, but I still sketched a rough outline of what I wanted the tower to look like. And my work, my part of this process, was complete. I turned the reigns over to my husband where he began to work his magic for his little girl. Okay. And his wife.

He drew. He chiseled. He sculpted. He cleaned up more tiny, white balls of Styrofoam then grains of sand at the sea. He spray-painted. He waited. He checked it. He spray-painted it some more and finally declared it was finished. And the result was more spectacular than I had imagined it would be. When book report day arrived, I helped my oldest into her princess gown, attached the extensive braid, verified she had her written copy of the book report, loaded the tower prop into the car, rehearsed with her how it would work best and headed to school.

If I could've stayed at the school to watch her, I probably would have. I couldn't wait to pick her up and hear how it went. And of course, see what the teacher thought of it. She loved it. Raved about it. And gave my daughter a perfect grade on it.

Flash forward to present day and our reminiscent post-dinner conversation. What wasn't perfect that night was my family's interpretation of it. As I began retelling the story, my daughter declared, "Oh yeah! I remember that! That's when Dad built that cool castle tower for the book report!" "Wait. What? Your Dad? Your Dad? I was the mastermind behind the whole thing and did most of the work, yet your Dad gets all the credit?"

In less time than it takes to blink, a fury of emotions welled up inside me. First to see the light of day was correction. Because clearly, my daughter's memory needed a minor tweaking. "Honey, I was the one who came up with that idea. I was the one who read the book.

I helped write the report. I was the one who made the braid. I was the one who found the materials. I was the one who told your father what to do with those materials. I was the one who got you dressed and took you to school so you could present your report. It wasn't just your Dad...dear."

Following quickly on the heels of correction was frustration. Then hurt. And anger. Bad went to worse when my husband chuckled lightheartedly and teasingly at the scene playing out and our middle daughter gave her two cents. Nobody got it. Nobody got that Mama wasn't happy. And as the familiar cliché reminds us, soon nobody else was happy either.

The happy hike down memory lane was left undone. Pushing my chair back from the table, I made my way to my bedroom, which may or may not have included some stomping and possibly dramatic door slamming for added effect. I brooded. I sulked. I wallowed. I told God to make them see it my way. Then I had to ask myself the hard question: Why did that situation trigger me? Why did my daughter's unintentional, completely innocent, declaration offend me so?

Turns out I don't like being ignored for what I do. I don't need my people to go bonkers and celebrate me all day, every day, for what I do. But I can certainly appreciate an intentional, grateful nod in my direction from time to time.

Apparently, and maybe even subconsciously, I also I expected my children would blissfully recall my active hand in their experiences over the years. This incident was a wake-up call that this would not be the case. I have absolutely no control over their perspectives and their translations of their childhood under my care. What they perceive, what they conjure up, what they treasure is entirely up to them.

My unvoiced, unmet expectations caused the night to go from sweet to sour in a flash. My people were confused and treaded timidly for the next hour or so while I retreated and licked my wounds. Unmet expectations can do that. They can wreak havoc on relationships. They can cause frustration and division. All become someone didn't pause to express their need or their want.

So that's what I did. I called my people in and apologized first. I asked for their forgiveness for the less-than- ideal way I handled my hurt. I asked them if they were open to hearing why I thought I'd come undone and if I could share my heart about why I believed I felt the way I felt. Their reaction was kind and tender.

Mercifully, they listened as I explained the treasure of hearing a simple "thank you" every now and then and how that one simple gesture burrows deep and blooms wide in a mama's heart. But the most noteworthy thing I walked away with that night is how stinking tough it is to die to self. Jesus Himself instructed a crowd and His own disciples to deny themselves, take up their cross, and follow Him (Mark 8:34). Dying to self is what Jesus did. It's what Christians are called to do. It's what good parents do for the children they love, right? I mean, I thought I'd done a fair job of living according to this principle over the years; God showed me otherwise. Jesus replied… "I tell you the truth, unless a kernel of wheat falls to the ground and dies, it remains only a single seed. But if it dies, it produces many seeds. The man who loves his life will lose it, while the man who hates his life in this world will keep it for eternal life. Whoever serves me must follow me; and where I am, my servant also will be. My Father will honor the one who serves me." John 12:23-26.

> He raises us to new life with Him and through Him. His life-breath resuscitates the dead and dry recesses of our hearts and minds.

I know I won't always get this right. I will fail and consequently be forced to endure "another lap around the desert" so to speak. I'm human. I'm weak. My flesh will always want to rise up, be seen, be noticed and be acknowledged. Dying daily to what I want doesn't come easily. Crucifying myself is hard. But praise God, there is a Helper, known as the Holy Spirit who comes alongside us, pointing us to the Son and making us more like Him. The One who set the supreme example for humility and for doing the hard things. One who doesn't scoff at our shortcomings, but bends low to aid us in our time of need. One who understands the desire for gratitude expressed, but doesn't demand it. One who isn't pushy, but undeniably deserves my acknowledgement and my many "thank-you's" for His hand in my life.

As we surrender our selfish, imperfect ways and will to His perfect way and will, the same power that resurrected Jesus from the dead resurrects us, too. He raises us to new life with Him and through Him. His life-breath resuscitates the dead and dry recesses of our hearts and minds. We experience transformation. Yes, on the initial moment of salvation and yes, as needed-- moment by moment in our daily lives.

The knowledge that His "power is made perfect in my weakness" (2 Corinthians 12:9) is one of my most favorite encouragements found in His Word. As a matter of fact, the Apostle Paul went on to state that because of the Lord's grace in this area, he could boast all the more gladly about his weaknesses, so that Christ's power might rest on him. I couldn't agree more. "For when I am weak, then I am strong" (2 Corinthians 12:10). Perfect power. Done. Particularly when my imperfect actions and my imperfect behavior result in me becoming perfectly undone with those I love most.

Lesson #4: Take notice of those silent expectations running around in your head and heart. Be brave to voice them to those you love. Walk in humility. It hurts far less when you fall.

Seven months. That's how long it took me to write this chapter for this book. Not because I excitedly jumped on it the second Karen emailed me about the opportunity. But because I was outright afraid. I used to write. I used to love to write. I used to write often. I felt inspired by what I saw, what I experienced and what God was teaching me, mostly through the lens of my family. But I stopped writing the year(s) following the conclusion of our adoption. Life was busy and hard. There was just too much noise in my life; it was good noise, but noise

> Lesson #4: Take notice of those silent expectations running around in your head and heart. Be brave to voice them to those you love. Walk in humility. It hurts far less when you fall.

nonetheless that seemed to drown out His still, small voice.

I was not soaking in His Word as I once had, was not praying down walls like I once had, was not giving a substantial voice to anything anymore. But mostly, I was afraid. Downright afraid of what God was going to ask me to do next. We had just come out of such a big, hard thing with the adoption and the coward in me just didn't want to hear the next big, (or little) hard thing on the list. I was afraid that I wouldn't be able to write enough to warrant a chapter. Afraid readers wouldn't connect with my style or my stories. Afraid the editor would rip it up and slap a big 'ol "NOPE" across my contribution. But mostly afraid that I would outright fall on my face and fail. I would fail at discerning His voice and fail at conveying that in words, on paper.

That intense fear of failure led this perfectionist to

procrastinate. I worried. I critiqued. I compared. I analyzed so much about doing it and not doing it well that it immobilized me. As a result, I failed to do any writing at all. For seven long months. "But thanks to be God! He gives us the victory through our Lord Jesus Christ!" (1 Corinthians 15:57).

You see, the numeral seven seems to be a favorite of God's. It is represented all throughout Scripture in biblical patterns, signifying completion, jubilation, and perfection. And seven months was the precise amount of time I needed for Him to display His perfect power both in me and through my weaknesses, fleshing out these thoughts, these stories, and these scriptures in authentic, meaningful ways for me and hopefully, for you, too.

> But in the wait, I was given the greatest gift: repeated affirmations of His presence with me, His provision for me, and His power within me.

I pummeled Him with questions during this time. And though I am confident He heard my cries, it seemed as if no tangible, audible replies were reciprocated to me. But in the wait, I was given the greatest gift: repeated affirmations of His presence with me, His provision for me, and His power within me. He would be with me. He would provide for me. He would empower me. I had seen Him move my fear-covered mountains before-- huge, looming, seemingly unconquerable mountains and I would see Him do it again.

I know Him as my faithful Father, who has yet to fail me. I have come to an even greater understanding that through my rational (or irrational) fear, my inconsistencies, my wanderings, my unfaithfulness and my imperfections, He will come through. He always does. For His glory and for our good. He can be trusted. And what He begins, He will bring to completion. Count on it.

Lesson #5: Get okay with waiting. He promises to renew your strength and infuse you with courage while you wait. Trust Him to keep His Word; He always does. When the fear of failure screams, "You don't have enough

_____ to accomplish this!" confidently scream back, "You're right. But my abundant God does through me!"

While I recognize and proudly wave the banner over the fact that perfectionists consistently get the job done, whatever it is, I have been learning that it's in this coming undone where real power and strength lie. I can work hard. I can see the imperfections and remedy them. I can rally the troops and keep scaling the mountain. But if I don't stop before I forge ahead, I am going to trip and fall flat on my face in self-effort and self-preservation. I must ask, and then allow, the Holy Spirit to untangle me from my own stumbling blocks, allowing my imperfections to pave a path to His perfect peace. He alone is worthy. If I haven't fallen on my face in worship because of that Truth, my view of Him is too faint and too dim. Becoming undone ruins us. It's in that realization that we see we are done for. On our own, we're defeated. We're doomed.

> Lesson #5: Get okay with waiting. He promises to renew your strength and infuse you with courage while you wait. Trust Him to keep His Word; He always does.

We're beaten and washed up apart from Him. The more I come undone, the better. The more I lose my own composure, the more His character is seen.

> When I release my desire to hold things in my tightly squeezed fists, the more opportunities there are for His power to be made perfect in my weaknesses and for His perfection to overshadow my imperfections.

When I release my desire to hold things in my tightly squeezed fists, the more opportunities there are for His power to be made perfect in my weaknesses and for His perfection to overshadow my imperfections. Less of me equals more of Him. For my weaknesses do not repel Him. Neither do yours. In fact, they are an open invitation for Him to draw near. To draw near and fill in the feeble areas with His all-encompassing strength.

It's best to leave these perfectionistic tendencies undone. It's best to let Him finish what He initiated and fulfill us to accomplish His perfect will in His perfect way.

It's best to own being catawampus from time to time.

Falling on our faces, whether in pride or humility, affords Him the privilege of doing what a loving parent does. He shows up by our side, in our moment of greatest need and scoops us up. He helps us. He shields us. He holds us in His perfect, love-filled embrace and takes great delight in us, His perfectly imperfect children, I might add.

Perfectly Imperfect
Study Guide

1. What were the 5 Lessons Michele shared?

    1._____

    2._____

    3._____

    4._____

    5._____

2. Choose two of the Lessons that spoke to you and share why.

Lesson #_____

_____

_____

_____

_____

_____

Lesson #_____

_____

_____

_____

3. Do you struggle with perfectionism? If so, write a prayer asking God to help you as you become "undone" and surrender the tight grip of perfectionism into His capable hands.

_____

_____

_____

_____

_____

_____

_____

_____

Heavenly Father, lovingly turn our eyes on you and not ourselves. Perfectionism steals our joy in serving you. May we serve you with your heart of love, not perfectionism. In Jesus' Name I Pray Amen.

This prayer was written and prayed over you by my amazing and Godly mom, Kathy Mutchler.

How to Battle instead of Dabble...

So, here we are. Together. Wondering how in the world do we win this battle of comparison? What's it going to take? How will we win? What do we need to do in order to be victorious here? Because, let's be real, we haven't done much winning in this area, wouldn't you agree? In the battle of comparison, I can tell you that most of us have a losing record. That record is almost as bad as the Atlanta Braves record in 1988 with a whopping 54-106. That is 54 wins and 106 losses. They lost almost twice as much as they won. I can relate to those stats. No one was lined up the next year to watch them play and I don't blame them. Losing stinks. But, guess what happened just a few years later in 1995? They won the World Series. They figured it out. They figured out how to win, and win they did. So, let's be "BRAVE" and battle, and win.

I've thought of just a few ways that we can battle this comparison trap. These aren't the only ways, mind you, so if you have discovered other helpful tips to battle comparison, please share with all your sisters...we need all the help we can get!

The first way we can battle this comparison trap is to recognize the enemy's tactics. We spent an entire chapter on him. The way he lies, how he works and manipulates. You may even be tired of talking about him and I understand that. But I'm also pretty sure you've figured out that I am very passionate about calling him out. I think one of the ways we combat the pull to compare is to recognize how he is trying to defeat us. We already know he is a liar, so let's start there. When you "hear" something in your heart or head, write it down. Seriously, write it down. SEE it. Then decide if it is the truth or if it is a lie. For example, if you hear, "You're not good at anything", write it down, see the sentence, then decide if that statement is really true. Ask yourself, "Does this sound like something *God* would say about me or does it sound like something *Satan* would say?" Ask yourself, "Why would Satan want me to believe this about myself?" and then ask, "Why would God want me to believe this about myself?" This is a good way to bring light to Satan's lies and not afford him the opportunity to sabotage us.

Not only is Satan a liar, but remember he wants us women to be at war with each other. He doesn't want an army to rise up, he wants the army to fight each other. Remember that quote, "Together we stand, divided we fall"? The enemy really is scared of the first part of that quote, "together we stand", so he works hard at the second, "divided we fall." When you have a thought or a comparison, ask yourself, "Is this going to bring division between that person and myself?" "Is this comparison going to make either of us better?" See, the enemy doesn't want you to ask any of these questions because he hates the answer...and he hates you. Always, and I mean always be ready to recognize Satan's tactics in this area.

> It's amazing what happens when we turn our comparisons into compliments.

Remember, he prowls, he seeks, he wants to devour. In order to win this battle, we need to be ready to see the enemy and his tactics. When we recognize that it's him, we can call him out and do battle effectively. Don't let him win.

Another way to battle instead of dabble, is to be an encourager. It's amazing what happens when we turn our comparisons into compliments. If we were honest, we could say that women are not the most encouraging or uplifting creatures around. We struggle with complimenting each other maybe because we feel like it diminishes us or even worse, it may actually make her feel good about herself for a second. Why do we think like that? Why do we resist offering another woman a compliment? Why is it so taboo? If we want to win this battle, we must learn the art of encouraging. Let's look at an example of just how to turn our comparison into a compliment. Several years ago, I had joined a gym. Normally, the gym is not a very safe and

> If we want to win this battle, we must learn the art of encouraging.

friendly place for women because there is so much judgement happening...judgement of one's self and of other women. The very fit women don't get talked to in the gym by other women. They get sneered at. There's this uncomfortable, unsaid, unhealthy treatment of those beautifully fit women. This particular day that I was at the gym, one of those beautifully fit women entered and began her workout. I could sense the climate around her...the stares, the negative body language from others, the frustration. She was stunning, ya'll. She had worked hard on her body and it showed. Nothing jiggled. Nothing was hanging out. It was all right where it was supposed to be. My first reaction was, well, the normal one. I immediately recognized my faults. I held up the chart in my head of what she looked like compared to what I looked like. Her quads to mine. Her shoulders to mine. How much she could lift compared to me etc. I was definitely on the losing side of that comparison and I felt every bit of that loss. But, in that moment, I felt Him say to me, "Encourage her. Tell her how great she looks." Well, let's just say that I wasn't a willing participant at first. I balked, dug my heels in and said, "Ummm...Lord, I am NOT doing that...no way." I did a few more sets of legs and knew I needed to obey. So, I walked over to her and tapped her on her rock hard, well-defined deltoid (her shoulder in layman's terms). She looked up at me, took her ear buds out, and arched her well-plucked eyebrows as if to say, "Can I help you?" I sucked in a breath and said, "Hey, I'm really sorry to bother your workout, but I just wanted to tell you how great you look. I'm not trying to be weird or anything, I just know you have worked hard, and it shows. You really look great." Her jaw dropped. She got herself together and said, "Wow...no woman has ever said that to me at the gym before. Thanks. I was looking at your legs earlier too...they are amazing!" I thanked her for her compliment and went back to my workout. My entire workout was different from that moment on. I was different. I felt so full and so very good. Not because she gave me a compliment about my legs but because I had taken the comparison that had plagued and defeated me and turned it into something totally different...something positive...something useful, and it felt amazing. Did she still have better quads than me? Yes. Did she still have more defined shoulders than me? Yep. Was she still lifting heavier than me? She sure was. Notice that nothing about the comparison chart had changed. The thing that had changed was that I took that comparison and turned it into a compliment and it did something great for her AND for me!

When we find ourselves in the middle of making a comparison, we have a choice. We can follow through with that comparison, take the data, and apply it, ever so despicably, to ourselves. Or, we can take that very thing that we are comparing and flip it into something good, better yet, something great.

The next time you have a co-worker who is really good at her job and you find yourself comparing how you measure up to her gifts and talents, pick one of those gifts and encourage her with it. Specifically call it out and let her know. Say, "Lisa, I just wanted to tell you that you are very good at the marketing side of this job!" Maybe it's a lady at church who is a gifted teacher and you always feel inadequate because her teaching is powerful. Say, "Donna, you are extremely gifted at communicating God's Word. Thank you for sharing your gift with us!" If you have a friend who is physically fit and you feel like Jabba the Hut next to her, you have a choice. You can listen to the Jabba the Hut talk, or, you can encourage her with something like, "Jackie, I know how hard you work to look as good as you do, I'm so proud of you!" Build her up and in doing so, you will build something even greater...your character.

I do want to point out something REALLY important here so please don't miss this. Did you notice that when I was giving the examples above, I gave the compliment but I never followed it with something negative about the giver of the compliment? For instance, the compliment for Lisa. It read, "Lisa, I just wanted to tell you that you are very good at the marketing side of this job!" You do not need to add, "Lisa, I just wanted to tell you that you are very good at the marketing side of this job! I'm terrible at it and wish I could be as good as you!" The compliment for Donna doesn't read, "Donna, you are extremely gifted at communicating God's Word. Thank you for sharing your gift with us! I have tried over and over to teach like you but I'm just so terrible at it." Compliment their gift without diminishing your own. There is no reason to throw yourself under the bus. In the same way, resist the desire to toot your own horn as you give the compliment. For example, "Donna, you are

> Compliment their gift without diminishing your own.

extremely gifted at communicating God's Word. Thank you for sharing your gift with us! I love to teach and have people confirm that gifting in me as well! Isn't it great!" This isn't about you validating yourself. It is about turning a comparison into a compliment.

1 Thessalonians 5:11 ESV says, "Therefore encourage one another and build one another up, just as you are doing." If we, as women, will set it in our hearts to choose to turn our comparisons into compliments and our issues into encouragements, we will be doing ourselves and each other a ginormous favor. This is how

we stop fighting each other and tearing each other down. We link arms and say, "You be great at what you are great at, and I'll be great at what I'm great at...sound good?" By turning that comparison into a compliment, we do two things. First, we stop the data of comparison from going any further in our heads and in our hearts. Second, we

> We link arms and say, "You be great at what you are great at, and I'll be great at what I'm great at...sound good?"

flip the focus off of us and onto someone else which is always a wise thing to do. So, be an *encourager.* Choose to battle instead of dabble by turning that comparison into an opportunity to compliment. You'll be surprised at just how effective this will be in the war of comparison.

Another way to battle this urge to compare is probably my most favorite...and the most difficult. We need to stop listening to ourselves and start talking to ourselves. Sounds strange doesn't it? Now, ya'll, I talk to myself ALL the time, out loud, in public, but it's not quite the same thing. Let me explain. Remember those lies that Satan throws our way? The ones that tell us we aren't good enough, pretty enough, smart enough, etc.? He is always the root of the lie, but sometimes we are the ones speaking it to our own hearts. We listen to ourselves say "You can't", or "You're not". We become our own worst enemy, don't we?

In this battle of making comparisons, we must begin *telling* ourselves the truth instead of *listening* to the lies. Do you know that David in the Bible had a similar struggle? Not so much in the art of comparison, but with listening to himself rather than telling. Guess what he did? He decided to do the talking instead of the listening. "Why, my soul, are you downcast? Why so disturbed within me? Put your hope in God, for I will yet praise him, my Savior and my God." Psalm 42:5. See, he was talking to himself, saying, "Why, soul, are you down? Why are you so disturbed?" Then he continues to tell himself what he needs to do next, "Put your hope in God!" David understood the importance of being the one doing the talking instead of the listening. We *listen* to lies. We *tell* ourselves the truth.

> In this battle of making comparisons, we must begin *telling* ourselves the truth instead of *listening* to the lies.

Not only do we need to begin talking to ourselves

instead of listening, but I believe that our "self-talk" needs an overhaul. How do you speak to yourself? What are some phrases that you frequently use? What are you telling yourself you are or are not? *Who* are you telling yourself you are or are not? It's amazing to me sometimes how I will speak to myself. Harsh. Cruel. Mean. Unforgiving. No grace. No mercy. No tolerance. Do you know the irony of this? I would NEVER talk to someone else that way. Never. And if someone else spoke to a person I love like that...well, let's just say I would struggle keeping myself together...well, honestly, there may be bail money involved...just saying. However, I often don't even think twice about telling myself horrible or negative things. We speak to ourselves worse than we speak to our own dogs and we've been okay with it, haven't we? After all, no one hears those things, do they? No one can hear what we say to ourselves so no one can hold us accountable. Well, until today. See, God hears all of it. He is privy to **all** of our self-talk. The good, the bad, and the ugly. He's calling it into account today. He doesn't speak to you like that. He doesn't want other people speaking to you like that and He certainly doesn't want you to speak to yourself that way.

Why is our "self-talk" so important? Well, often it's the first thing we hear when we wake up and the last thing we hear when we go to bed, isn't it? What we tell ourselves matters because we matter. You matter. Some of you have let your "self-talk" turn into "stinking thinking". Everything is negative. Everything you tell yourself involves what is wrong with you. What you aren't. What you can't do. Beloved, please understand that what you tell yourself is important...more important than you may think. Why? Because what you tell yourself, you listen to. And what you listen to, you believe. And what you believe about yourself determines how you live your life.

So, what should we be telling ourselves? What should we be listening to? Philippians 4:8-9 The Message, "Summing it all up, friends, I'd say you'll do best by filling your minds and meditating on things true, noble, reputable, authentic, compelling, gracious; the best, not the worst; the beautiful, not the ugly; things to praise, not things to curse..." The NIV says it this way, "Finally, brothers and sisters,

> Because what you tell yourself, you listen to. And what you listen to, you believe. And what you believe about yourself determines how you live your life.

whatever is true, whatever is noble, whatever is right, whatever is pure, whatever is lovely, whatever is admirable--if anything is excellent or praiseworthy-- think about such things." There is so much meat in this verse on how to help us navigate how we talk to ourselves and manage our "stinking thinking".

Imagine if we really filled our minds with things that are true, authentic, and gracious. Can you even contemplate what would happen if we meditated on the best about us instead of the worst? Or if we concentrated on what was beautiful about ourselves instead of what we thought was ugly? Can you even fathom what it would look like to find things to praise about ourselves instead of choosing things to curse? Oh, dear one, this would be life-changing for us, wouldn't it? This could possibly change EVERYTHING for you and for me.

It has become clear to me that in order to battle the desire to compare, I must battle what I tell myself. What I choose to listen to. What I allow myself to believe *about* myself. We must choose to talk to ourselves instead of listening to ourselves and those things we tell ourselves **must** be good. They **must** be worthy. They **must** be the truth. And we know that the truth will set us free indeed!

The last way I believe we can fight this battle of comparison is to recognize the enormous influence the media has had in this war. Internet images, magazines, Facebook, Instagram, Snapchat, billboards...the list goes on. Want to know what all these things have in common? Airbrush, Photoshop, filters, special angles and everything in between, that's what. They have given us

> We must choose to talk to ourselves instead of listening to ourselves and those things we tell ourselves **must** be good. They **must** be worthy. They **must** be the truth. And we know that the truth will set us free indeed!

such unrealistic images to live up to and in doing so, they have slayed every woman that doesn't have a twenty-four inch waist or no thigh gap. The average model is 5'9 and weighs 110 pounds. How many of us can live up to that? Stylists take hours and hours to make the celebrities photo-worthy and then they *still* get photoshopped! I recently read about some famous women who are fighting back when it comes to the facade of no cellulite, no acne, and little thighs. Lady Gaga was not pleased with her December 2013 Glamour cover, which she felt was heavily airbrushed. When Gaga was honored at the Glamour Woman of the Year Awards, she took the opportunity to blast the magazine for its overuse of Photoshop. "I felt my skin looked too perfect. I felt my hair looked too soft," the "Bad Romance" singer said. "I do not look like this when I wake up in the morning... I don't even look like this," referring to her wild wig and makeup for the evening. She went on to say that she thought Photoshop was damaging to readers who see the images and called on her fans to "fight back against the forces that make them feel like they're not beautiful." She also issued a challenge to the media: "It is fair to write about the change in your magazines. But what I want to see is the change on your covers... When the covers change, that's when culture changes." Another young actress, Zendaya, posted on her Instagram, "Had a new shoot come out today and was shocked when I found my 19 year old hips and torso quite manipulated. These are the things that make women self-conscious, that create the unrealistic ideals of beauty that we have. Anyone who knows who I am knows I stand for honest and pure self-love. So I took it upon myself to release the real pic and I love it???? Thank you @modelistemagazine for pulling down the images and fixing this retouch issue."

The media is perpetuating this ideal of perfection, beauty, and of what every woman is "supposed" to look like. Ph.D. Romeo Vitelli wrote in Psychology Today, "Content analysis of female characters show a bias towards body weights well below the recommended size and weight for people in their age group. As a result, adolescent females who are unable to conform to the ideal being put forward by movie and television find themselves taking extreme measures to be more like their role models. With thinness presented as the ideal body shape and a necessary prerequisite for health and happiness, anyone falling short of this ideal is vulnerable to depression, poor self-esteem, and general body dissatisfaction. The effect of media content on ideas of physical beauty appears remarkably robust with women reporting greater feelings of inadequacy regardless of their real body weight."

What does this have to do with us and our battle in the desire to compare? Well, a lot actually. We are constantly being bombarded with these images that we know we can't live up to. It's frustrating. Like, really frustrating. It has conditioned us, along with our own humanness, to look at every woman through the lens of comparison. And the interesting thing is that since we feel like we can't measure up to the beauty on the cover of the magazine, at least we look better than that soccer mom or that co-worker. Here's what I'm asking us to do, recognize this MAJOR flaw in the media, the fashion industry, and whatever other avenue this can take. Recognize it and call it out so we will not fall victim to it any longer. We've been conditioned to compare and then take those comparisons to others. I made a promise to myself several years ago that when I saw a beautiful, flawless woman on the cover of a magazine or her picture on the internet, I would say to myself, "Self, you would look like that too if you were airbrushed and photoshopped." For some reason, that's all it takes for me to snap back into reality. See, reality is, those women have cellulite. They have acne. Their eyebrows may be a bit funky. Their stomach may not be that flat or their smile that white. I can pass over their perfect images because I know that they are NOT perfect. This recognition seems to help me, it focuses me, it brings me back. I do my best battling when I recognize what I'm fighting against...and what I'm fighting against is Photoshop.

As I said at the beginning of this chapter, these are just a few ways to battle instead of dabble. Some of you precious sisters have already found what works for you, what helps you fight this desire to compare. I stand and applaud you, dear one. Now, go share it with another sister. Help her with her battle. Equip her with ammo to fight the enemy. In my journey, I feel like I battle the best when I am quick to recognize Satan and his ways, call it out, and speak truth to it. I find success when I turn comparison into compliments. Shifting the focus onto her strengths minimizes the desire to pay attention to what I think my weaknesses may be. I must talk to myself instead of

[Unrealistic expectations cannot rule me.]

listening to myself. I need to tell myself the truth instead of listening to the lies. And when I DO talk to myself, it must be the things that Philippians 4:8 talks about. And lastly, it is so important for me to recognize the media's role in this battle. Unrealistic expectations cannot rule me. I refuse to think that woman on the cover, or that model on Instagram is any reflection of what I am to be. None of these ways are easy, mind you. If they were, the title to this chapter would not have the word "battle" in it, right? It is a battle. It *is* a war. My prayer is that this chapter will help equip you with tools and ammo to help you win!

How to Battle
Instead of Dabble
Study Guide

1. List the ways given to help battle the desire to compare.

    * _____

    * _____

    * _____

    * _____

2. Which one of these do you think will come more easily to you? Why? _____

_____

_____

_____

3. Which one of these might be hard for you? Why?

_____

_____

_____

_____

_____

_____

_____

4. Write out Philippians 4:8 and share how it can help you with your "self-talk" or "stinking thinking".

_____

_____

_____

_____

_____

_____

_____

"Father, Abba, my Daddy, would You be with my sisters as they allow the truths of this chapter to penetrate through any lies that the enemy has sought to embed in their hearts, their minds, their souls. May they begin to recognize the tactics of the enemy and wage war on him! As they seek to actually write down what they hear in their mind, SPEAK to it Daddy. Show them the Truth of Your Word. Show them what You say about them, that they are fearfully and wonderfully made, that there is a purpose and plan for their lives and that You want them thinking on what is true, noble, right, pure, lovely, admirable, excellent and praiseworthy. May we stand united and recognize the power of lifting one another up with words of life, words of encouragement, words of wisdom. Allow us to see the individual attractiveness and uniqueness of one another without diminishing our own beauty that You've given to us. We are a tapestry of Your glory, meant to compliment one another as You weave our lives together in love, in grace, in forgiveness, in seasons and out of seasons, in ministry, in friendships, ALL of it for the purpose of reflecting Jesus, His exquisite beauty, displayed in our woven and intertwined lives. Let us be ready to speak rather than listen when the enemy chooses to whisper those lies that have so easily entangled us. No more. We stand united, committed to protect one another rather than destroy. Renew our minds. Teach us to love ourselves. Guide our words spoken in the quiet of our own minds.

Use us to be a source of strength, of love, of encouragement, of accountability to one another. May we stand together against the message of this world, with its deceit of what beauty is. The world screams the claims of perfection, one mold that says, "You must be this size, look this way, have this hair, wear these clothes" ALL LIES. WE serve a God of unmatched beauty and unique creativity, He loves our differences, He made us that way, may we bend our ear to Him and allow Him to show us the significance of our differences, that there is purpose in it, the differences are necessary and used by Him for His glory and Divine direction to accomplish His plan. When you gaze upon a sunset, it's the contrast of colors that make it breathtaking. Same with His daughters, it's the contrast, the differences that make us breathtaking. Hold fast to His declaration over you and the strength there is when unity reigns among His daughters. Resist the desire to compare, recognizing it is the enemy's trap to destroy you and your sister. I ask all this in Jesus name and seal it in His blood. Amen!"

This prayer was written and prayed over you by my beautiful sister Veronica Sanders.

What If...?

That's a loaded question isn't it? The sentence doesn't even need to be finished but yet it sends fear ripping through our hearts. We hate "what if's" don't we? You don't have to live long to realize that "what if's" are a part of life and they show up all the time. The realm of comparison is no different. We are going to take this chapter to discuss some of the "what if's" in the comparison game. So...what if..?

What if...

What if you've never struggled with the comparison trap...until now? Maybe you've spent your whole life happily avoiding the game that most of us have lost in. Or, maybe you have been able to steer clear of any comparison hang-ups all throughout your life. But then, it all crashes down on you and you suddenly find yourself smack dab in the middle of it. The comparison; the ups, the downs, the highs and the lows…mostly the lows. Maybe you're like the woman who said to me, "I've NEVER dealt with comparison…until now and I'm in my FORTIES! What is going on"? She specifically asked me to address all of you who did not struggle with comparison previously, but now do.

So, I started thinking, really thinking, about what would cause a "non-comparer" to start comparing? Do you go to bed on a Tuesday night a "non-comparer" but wake up on Wednesday morning a "comparer"? Do you all of a sudden go from "confident in that" to "no-longer-confident in that?" Now, remember, I'm no psychologist, counselor, or theologian, so all of this is just my opinion, my perspective, and my belief. I think there may be a couple of reasons this may happen.

First, I think the late onset of comparison can happen in you when you experience a life-changing event. Something BIG has happened. So big that your life will never be the same again. Possibly a death, a birth, a move, a new job, the loss of a job, a marriage, a divorce, etc. These types of events can sometimes catapult someone into comparison. Why? Well, maybe because everything in your life looks different now. It wasn't what it USED to be, therefore, it presents new obstacles or opportunities for insecurities to creep in. You begin looking at things differently because things ARE different. This may open doors for comparison to start to invade where it once was never welcomed before.

Another reason I think you can struggle with comparison later in life is because you've had longer to actually live in this world. The longer we live, the more time we have to experience the opportunity to compare. Somewhere down the line you may have allowed a lie to sneak in and stay. That lie quickly turns into a desire to look around and compare. Say you've never really been tempted to look at another woman and compare yourself to her. Then, you hit forty. You begin to see wrinkles in the mirror. You see the gray roots. You see the saggy stuff...and there are a lot of things that could fit in that category. I remember reading a story about an older woman. She was sharing that when she got out of the shower, she had a shooting pain in her chest. She was fairly confident that she was having a heart attack with the amount of pain that she was experiencing. She looked down only to realize that she was standing on her boob. See...saggy stuff. You see all of the signs of aging and then you see the twenty-two year old. No wrinkles. No gray roots. No saggy stuff. Then, it happens. Comparison. It's all downhill from there...just like your boobs.

Maybe that's why it feels like there's a sudden onset of comparison. Whether a huge life event or just living long enough, it seems like it could happen. I'd suggest utilizing the chapter on how to battle instead of dabble to help combat this new journey.

What if...

What if you feel like you have a handle on your comparison woes and then all of a sudden, out of the blue, WHAM, it hits you and you fall right back in to that deep, nasty, comparison trap? Been there...fallen in that. In fact it's actually pretty common. You work hard to combat the battle that wages within you when it comes to comparison. Whether it's comparing yourself to yourself OR comparing yourself to someone else, you're working hard to do what is necessary to be victorious in it. And then...in a blink of an eye, you feel like you've been ambushed. Two steps forward. 14,502 steps back. That's how it feels anyway, doesn't it?

I know this feeling all too well. I recently felt like I was winning this battle of Me vs. Me. I felt like I was moving forward in what God was showing me on how hard I was on myself with my weight gain and how I looked. I was letting Him speak to my heart about grace and embracing the beauty of "Now" as opposed to grieving the "Then". I was doing really well. I was impressing my own self (humble huh?). And then, one day while I was at the gym, I caught a glimpse of myself in the mirror while I was on the treadmill. The huge, huge, huge, mirror. My reflection stared back at me. Ya'll, I DOVE head-first into the pit. I couldn't breathe. You'd think that I would stop looking at the mirror right? Wrong. I kept glancing...hoping it would look different, that *I* would look different. But nope, no such luck. With all that the Lord had been teaching me and showing me, you'd think that I could have just stepped over that whole scene and been like, "God's been doing a work in me on grace and I will not let the enemy win. Nope, not today Satan. Get thee behind me." But I couldn't. I felt like when I told Satan to get behind me, he got on the treadmill with me and just said, "Well...you should see it from this angle...it ain't no better." Ugh. Double ugh.

So, what do we do when we get blind-sided? Well, I can tell you what I have to do and it comes from 2 Corinthians 10:5 (NLV) "We break down every thought and proud thing that puts itself up against the wisdom of God. We take hold of every thought and make it obey

Christic." The New International Version uses the phrase "take captive every thought". So, in those moments where comparison and all that it brings, blind-sides me, I have to break down those thoughts, take them captive, and make them obey Christ. What does that look like in real life? Well, that day at the gym when I caught the unflattering glimpse of myself reflected in the mirror, I had a couple of choices. I could choose to go down the road of self-pity and self-loathing or I could take those negative thoughts captive and make them obedient to Christ. How did I take them captive? I called them out. In my head and my heart I said, "I'm diving in the pit because of what I saw when I looked in the mirror. I didn't like the way I looked and the guilt, shame, and disappointment is overwhelming me." This is how you take your negative thoughts captive. Call them out; recognize them; unveil them. Then, you must make them obedient to Christ.

> So, in those moments where comparison and all that it brings, blind-sides me, I have to break down those thoughts, take them captive, and make them obey Christ.

How do you do that? You remind yourself of what God says. God told me that I was enough. God told me that in this particular season I was to extend grace to myself. God told me that He was doing something greater IN me and that soon it would show up on the OUTSIDE of me. I had to make my negative thoughts obey what the Lord had already said.

I think we can expect to get blind-sided or ambushed every now and then. We are human and we are flawed. Even though we may be presently walking in victory in this area, we can experience these moments of faltering and it's okay. It's OKAY! Take those thoughts captive and make them obedient to what God says about you. For me, I had to get back on the treadmill and keep going. I also had to tell Satan to get off...and to keep his opinions about my backside to himself.

What if...

What if *you* are the person other people compare themselves to? There are two sides to comparison, correct? The person comparing and the person they are comparing themselves to. Well, what happens when you are being used as the measuring stick? A young mom recently asked me this question. She was truly upset and frustrated. She said, "I really don't know what to do.

Women keep saying that I'm "supermom" and that it looks like I have a perfect life and have it all together. I am just trying to do the best I can with my family, but I'm not trying to make any other woman feel bad about how she's doing it. I feel like I can't win." This got me to thinking. Should this mom feel bad for giving her best to her family because other people are comparing themselves to her and they feel inadequate? Should this mom NOT give her best so it doesn't offend or hurt another mom? No, she shouldn't. She shouldn't feel guilty or stop giving her best because other women are comparing themselves to her. 1 Corinthians 10:31 says, "So, if you eat or drink or whatever you do, do everything to honor God." This mom should do whatever she is doing for the honor and glory of God. Whether it is making gourmet cupcakes for her child's class, being the PTO president, or putting makeup on every single morning for the car rider line. The pressure she feels because she is giving her best isn't coming from the Lord, it's coming from a human, and we humans are flawed.

So, if you are like this young mom, and you are doing your best as an offering to God but feel the pressure from your "friends" to take it down a notch, what should you do? Check out The Message version of the verse mentioned above. "So eat your meals heartily, not worrying about what others say about you—you're eating to God's glory, after all, not to please them. As a matter of fact, do everything that way, heartily and freely to God's glory. At the same time, don't be callous in your exercise of freedom, thoughtlessly stepping on the toes of those who aren't as free as you are. I try my best to be considerate of everyone's feelings in all these matters; I hope you will be, too." Do you see the balance here? Do

> The pressure she feels because she is giving her best isn't coming from the Lord, it's coming from a human, and we humans are flawed.

your thang. Slay your life. Be the best. Give the best. But, in doing so, be thoughtful and considerate of those who aren't killing it. Those who aren't slaying it. The ones who are struggling to keep their heads above water. Now, is that your fault? Is that your problem? No, it's not. But we are called to be thoughtful towards those people. The word "thoughtful" means to show consideration for the needs of other people. How do you do that? How can you continue honoring God with your best as you live but still be mindful of those around you who are struggling with insecurity and inadequacies?

•Be Real

Seriously, be real. If that means you are rockin' the mom game that day then great. But, if it's one of those days where you've lost your marbles with the kids, spilled dinner on the floor, snipped at your husband, and re-washed the weird smelling laundry for the fifth time…then own it and be real. When your friend asks how the day went, be honest. Don't sugar-coat it for her sake, or yours. I'm not telling you to go shouting to the whole world all your failures and dirty laundry (pun intended). What I'm saying is that it's okay to be real with those around you. Even though you may be giving your best and slaying life, no one is perfect. We may not mean to give off the impression that we are perfect or our life is perfect, **but sometimes we do.** Being real helps bring clarity to that assumption.

•Be Relatable & Approachable

If other women see you as not having ANY problems at all, you become un-relatable. And when you become un-relatable, you also become ineffective at reaching those women. Ineffective at reaching those women for Christ and encouraging them in their walk with Him. My eyes were opened to this truth when a friend and I were talking one day. I don't even remember the meat of the conversation but I remember her saying to me, "You do realize that's how other women see you right? Like you have it all together. Like you don't have any hang-ups or struggles." My reaction was an interesting one. It was a half-laugh, half-snort, half-choke. Hearing someone else who I trusted tell me that was eye opening. I guess I kind of knew that women saw me like that and if I were completely honest, I didn't mind it so much. "Let them think that!" I thought, "I know the truth. I'm on the hot mess express!" But God used that to open my eyes...and my heart. If I wanted to reach women for the Lord, and I desperately did, then I was going to have to be better at being real and relatable. Instead of using stories about other people's struggles in my teaching, I started using my own. I had plenty. I began sharing my struggles, even if they were small. Do you know what I found? I found that I became approachable to women and they began coming to me and I was able to minister to them. Women were no longer afraid I'd judge them because they didn't have it all together. They were no longer scared that I wouldn't understand their struggle. So they began opening up and I got the very thing I had always hoped for...the opportunity to reach women.

•Re-direct the attention

When your life appears perfect to others or it seems as if you have it all together, you will undoubtedly receive attention from others. Why? Well, because it isn't the norm. Some women will immediately compare and go down that road and some women will offer their praise or compliments concerning this incredible feat. Either one brings attention to you. So, what do you do with all that? What do you do with the attention that comes with doing something well? Do what Gideon did. Gideon was a military leader in the Old Testament and eventually became a Judge and a prophet. God Himself called Gideon a "mighty warrior" even though Gideon didn't believe it about himself. I'm thankful for a God who sees things in us before WE see it or believe it, aren't you? God told Gideon that he was to take his men into battle against the Midianites and that Gideon and his army would win. If you have a few minutes, this story is definitely worth taking the time to read in Judges 6, 7, and 8. Ironically, I find a lot of myself in Gideon. You may too. So, Gideon takes three hundred men to fight this army and it would be fair to say that the numbers were not even. "The Midianites, the Amalekites, and all the other eastern peoples had settled in the valley, thick as locusts. Their camels could no more be counted than the sand on the seashore." Judges 7:12 Gideon's three hundred men against the other army's "thick as locusts" and "tons of camels". Seemed like a very lopsided battle. It was. Gideon won bigtime. That's what happens when God leads you to the battle. He fights for you and He wins. Every.single.time. When the battle was ensuing, Gideon sent for other soldiers to catch anyone who was fleeing to the Jordan River. Two men, Zebah and Zalmunna, were among those soldiers

> That's what happens when God leads you to the battle. He fights for you and He wins. Every.single.time.

and they brought the heads of the opposing army leaders to Gideon. I guess it's kind of like when your cat brings you the bird it has killed. Not a big fan of dead birds or people's actual heads, but whatever. So, here these two men stood (well, I guess there was four if you count the two heads) in front of Gideon who had just defeated an army of the multitudes. Gideon was a winner. He did good. He was a champion. But listen to what these two guys said, "Now the Ephraimites asked Gideon, "Why have you treated us like this? Why didn't you call us when you went to fight Midian?" And they challenged him vigorously." Nice huh? Here Gideon takes on a bazillion soldiers and defeats them and these two knuckleheads fuss at him because he didn't call them sooner. Gideon succeeds, he does the "right" thing, yet he gets negative attention because of it. Ever happened to you? Maybe you brought those awesome spider cupcakes to your kid's school and you got an eye-roll from another mom. Maybe you posted the yummy roast with all your family sitting down for an evening meal on Facebook and you get replies like, "I wish I had the time to cook like that", or "You are supermom and super-wife, I could never keep up with you!" Maybe you work out every day to keep your body healthy yet you hear, "Well, I wish I had time to work out but I don't. I'll just stay fat" or "I have a job. I can't work out." You get the picture. It's attention for whatever it is that you are doing "well" or to the best of your ability. So, what did Gideon do? Well, let me say that he did much better than what my flesh would have done. Let's just say there would no longer be only TWO heads lying in front of me. I believe I would have doubled my investment. Just sayin. However, Gideon did it differently than I would have. Look at his response. "But he answered them, "What have I accomplished compared to you? Aren't the gleanings of Ephraim's grapes better than the full grape harvest of Abiezer? God gave Oreb and Zeeb, the Midianite leaders, into your hands. What was I able to do compared to you?" At this, their resentment against him subsided." Ohhhhhh…he's good isn't he? Do you see what he did there? He re-directed the attention. He was basically saying that these two men were the ones to cut the heads of the leaders, not Gideon. They deserved the praise, the accolades, and the attention. He was diverting the good he had done with the good they had done. Pretty wise huh? We can learn from him, friend. When that attention, good or bad, comes your way for doing something well, divert it. Proverbs 15:1 says, "A gentle response diverts anger, but a harsh statement incites fury." Even if the attention isn't considered in "anger", diverting it is always a great practice and yields a great result.

You may be reading all of this and think, "Why do I have to do all the work when it's the other people who have the problem? They are the one's comparing themselves to me?" Good question. The answer isn't any easier to swallow though. Because God asks you to, that's why. Whether it's positive attention for being great at life, or negative attention for the same reason, you have to step out in maturity. Be real, relatable, approachable, and re-direct the attention…and keep slaying life.

What if...?

Study Questions

1. Could you relate to any of the "What if's?" Which one(s) and how can you relate?

_____

_____

_____

_____

_____

2. Do you have a "What if?" of your own?

_____

_____

_____

_____

_____

_____

_____

3. In your opinion, how does being real, relatable, approachable, and re-directing attention help when someone may seem like they are perfect or have it all together?

_____

_____

_____

_____

_____

_____

Dear God,

A beautiful woman sits before you reading this book. As she reads to discover more about herself, You whisper to her heart, "You are chosen. You are mine. And you are enough! " Father, she seeks You, but You have already sought her before she was ever born. You have called her to intimacy with You so that You can share Your truths to her heart of who she is, instead of her thoughts of what she is not.

She is Your daughter, Your child, the one that You love more than her heart can comprehend. She is beautiful and special. Your word tells her that " *Your* divine power has given *her* everything required for life and godliness through the knowledge of *You* who called *her* by *Your* own glory and goodness." (2 Peter 1:3, emphasis mine) You have equipped her with all that she needs. You have fashioned her inside and out. She is "wonderfully made", and she is stunning!

I pray that she will see herself in Your eyes and that she will no longer struggle with comparison. Teach her Lord to bring her thoughts captive to You. Teach her to abide in Your Word so that she will know the truth and not believe the enemy's lies that make her feel unworthy. Father, show her Your love and the special gifts that You have equipped her with for everything she needs as a woman, a wife, a mom, and a friend. Show her how to celebrate the treasures that you have given her and not compare to others of anything that she may think that she is lacking. Teach her to use those gifts for Your glory and Your desires. Help her to be content with who she is in You and fulfilled in the beauty of the life that You have given her.

Lord, no matter what age or what stage of life that she is in, I pray that You will use her to draw her family and friends to You. I pray that You will teach her to share her life so that she is relatable and approachable to others. And most of all, Lord, as she reads every word on the next few pages, I pray that she will hear Your voice speak directly to her heart, just like the beautiful message of the Song of Solomon, "You are loved, and you are Mine."

This prayer was written and prayed over you by my friend, Rhonda Stamey, who has a deep passion to equip women with the Truth of His Word.

The Gold Standard

I've spent this ENTIRE book explaining to you that comparison is a thief. A liar. A killer. A destroyer. Have you gotten that truth yet? Well, for this next chapter, forget everything I've said about comparison. Forget every negative word. Every warning. Every paragraph bashing comparison. Forget it all. Every.single.word.of.it. Sounds pretty crazy doesn't it? Well, you'll just have to trust me for a minute, okay?

Do you know what a plumb line is? I didn't. There is a small problem with not knowing what one is…I was supposed to be using one…like every day. Ooppsss! A plumb line is defined as a piece of string with a weight attached to the end which is used to check if something such as a wall is vertical or that it slopes at the correct angle. Now, I'm not building walls mind you, but I am supposed to be using a plumb line in my life. And so are you. Amos 7:7-8 NLT "Then he showed me another vision. I saw the Lord standing beside a wall that had been built using a plumb line. He was using a plumb line to see if it was still straight. And the LORD said to me, "Amos, what do you see?"

I answered, "A plumb line."

And the Lord replied, "I will test my people with this plumb line..."

A plumb line. A standard. A measure. A yardstick. "Waaiitttt a minute!" you might be shouting, "YOU SAID THERE WAS NO YARDSTICK! You said we're NOT supposed to MEASURE ourselves to anyone else. You said..." Yes, I am very aware of what I've said. But forget it. Just for a minute anyway. See, there actually IS a comparison that is worth making. There actually IS a measuring stick. There is a standard. A Gold Standard. His name is Jesus Christ.

Jesus is the "Gold Standard" because, let's face it, we ALL want gold don't we? Remember those little, shiny, gold stars your teacher used to give you in class? I remember being so proud when my teacher would put one of those things on my paper. My shoulders would straighten up. I sat taller in my seat. My smile would stretch across my face. That gold star was the epitome of success! Silver stars were okay, but there was no substitute for the gold ones. Gold is the "color" of winners. Olympians strive to get the gold. A silver or bronze finish is just a reminder that they didn't get the gold. Trophies are gold...well, at least they are gold plated anyway. Some people even get gold teeth! Gold IS the standard. Gold IS what everyone longs for, shoots for, aims for. Well, this is no different. Christ is our Gold Standard.

When God sent His Son to earth, it was our opportunity to see a perfect example of what humanity should look like. Jesus was the living, breathing, model for how we should walk this earth. HE is our measuring stick. HE is our scale. HE is our mirror. It's important to note that Christ only did the will of His Father. So, in essence, both God the Father and Jesus the Son are one and are our examples of how to live. In John 10:30 Jesus states, "I and the Father are one." In the following verses, the Bible explains how we are to follow the example set before us:

Ephesians 5:1-2 "Therefore be imitators of God, as beloved children; and walk in love, just as Christ also loved you and gave Himself up for us, an offering and a sacrifice to God as a fragrant aroma."

1 Peter 2:21 "To this you were called, because Christ suffered for you, leaving you an example, that you should follow in his steps."

1 John 2:6 "Whoever claims to live in him must live as Jesus did."

Well, it's pretty clear that we are to imitate Christ as He is the standard to which we are held. He is the ultimate comparison. So, the next time you have the itch to compare, the desire to see where you fit on the sliding scale, or to see if you measure up, use Christ as your measuring stick. Determine where you stand when you stand next to Him. Gauge your morality against the One who created it. Evaluate your beauty compared to the most beautiful person to ever walk the earth. Talk about perspective. Talk about humbling.

What happens when we compare ourselves to Jesus? What do we find when we play *this* comparison game? We find a lot...some good and some bad...but all worth knowing.

•We find that we fall short.

This is kind of a no-brainer isn't it? Of course we will fall short. Like REALLY short. But, just in case you are wondering why we fall so short when we compare ourselves to Christ, it's pretty simple. Romans 3:23 says, "…for all have sinned and fall short of the glory of God". That word, "all" means, well, ALL but One. Hebrews 4:15 shares, "For we do not have a high priest who is unable to empathize with our weaknesses, but we have one who has been tempted in every way, just as we are—yet he did not sin." The high priest that is talked about here is Jesus.

So, the next time you have the itch to compare, the desire to see where you fit on the sliding scale, or to see if you measure up, use Christ as your measuring stick.

The One. We ALL have sinned, except for Christ. He was without sin. Perfect and blameless. I can't live up to that. Neither can you. No matter how hard we try, it can't happen. If you were to make a list of your attitudes, thoughts, and actions and compare them to

Jesus, what would happen? This idea actually makes me laugh a little. It's so futile. It's like cleaning your house while your toddlers are awake. Or like brushing your teeth while eating Oreos. Futile. But humor me, just for a minute, and think about it. If you were to measure your attitudes, thoughts, and actions and compare them to Christ, how would you fair? I can tell you that I would fail. Just like I did 8th grade algebra. Miserably, in fact. For instance, Philippians 2:5 says, "Your attitude should be the same as that of Christ Jesus." Sometimes I don't like reading the Bible. This is one of those times. I'm supposed to have the SAME attitude as Jesus? Okay, I totally do that. Well, sometimes I do that. Ummm…every now and then I do that. So….maybe…rarely I do that. Ugghhh, who am I kidding. More times than not, my attitude stinks. Stinks like the shorts after your teenager has played soccer in them for two weeks straight. Stinks like the unidentified moldy leftovers in the fridge. Stinks like…well, I think you get the picture. It just stinks. My attitude compared to Jesus' attitude? I'll let the stinky shorts speak for themselves. No one likes to fall short or to not measure up and that's understandable, but in this case, it's okay. It's okay because it is completely *impossible* for us to be perfect. It is completely *impossible* for us to be without sin. I know this sounds depressing or

> On our BEST day we could never come close to Jesus and His perfection. We will *always* fall short…and that is okay.

discouraging, but in all actuality, it should bring relief. On our BEST day we could never come close to Jesus and His perfection. We will *always* fall short…and that is okay. We may fall short, but we will inevitably fall into Him….and He will catch us every time.

•We find a target.

Jesus was perfect. Absolutely perfect. "And having been made perfect, He became to all those who obey Him the source of eternal salvation" Hebrews 5:9. Perfection. Well, if you haven't figured it out yet, you can't be perfect. Perfectly imperfect, yes, but just plain 'ol perfect, no.

What does this mean for us? We know we can't be perfect so now what? We aim high. That's right. We aim high. 2 Corinthians 13:11 says, "Aim for perfection…And the God of love and peace will be with you." Perfection is out of the question, but we still aim for it. Shoot for it. Go in the direction of it. Why? You might be thinking that it is a ridiculous waste of energy and effort to aim for a perfection that we will never be able to achieve. I hear ya sister, I do, but see, there's more to it. W. Clement Stone wrote, "Aim for the moon. If you miss, you may hit a star." The idea behind aiming for perfection is that the AIM is the goal. Not perfection. We are setting our sights and aiming high. Vince Lombardi, one of the greatest coaches in NFL history said, "Perfection is not attainable, but if we chase perfection we can catch excellence." It's the aim that counts. The direction in which we are going that will make the difference.

Perfection cannot be achieved. Excellence can. I've always been so frustrated with the phrase, "Practice makes perfect".

> The idea behind aiming for perfection is that the AIM is the goal. Not perfection.

Probably because it was said as I was dreading practicing a flute that I would never be good at. Me, playing the flute, be perfect? Yeah, well, we ALL knew that wasn't happening. You could have just asked those around me who had to hear me "practice". Several years later I heard the phrase that I liked much better, "Practice makes progress." Yes, yes it does. Progress, not perfection. The forward progress and movement as we strive for excellence. Hans Wrang writes, "Strive for perfection and you are at risk of getting dragged down by the thought that no matter what you do, you will never get there. Strive for excellence and every day you will see the results of your pursuits as you focus on the incremental improvement you have achieved."

When we compare ourselves to Christ, The Gold Standard, we find our target. We find which way to aim. Then, we shoot. Our lives then become a pursuit of excellence. Growth. Forward motion. What does that look like? This idea of aiming for perfection and chasing excellence? It reminds me of what the apostle Paul was talking about in Philippians 3:12-14 (NLV), "I do not say that I have received this or have already become perfect. But I keep going on to make that life my own as Christ Jesus made me His own. No, Christian brothers, I do not have that life yet. But I do have one thing. I forget everything that is behind me and look forward to that which is ahead of me. My eyes are on the crown. I want to win the race and get the crown of God's call from heaven through Christ Jesus." See, if we don't have a target in sight, to gaze upon, to go towards, then which way would we go? How would we know what to aim for? Comparing ourselves to Christ and His perfection sets us up for finding our target. We aim high to find our journey towards excellence. Excellence in our efforts toward our jobs, our families, our relationships, and our walk with Him. Aim for perfection. You will miss, no doubt, but in doing so, you chase something far more attainable…excellence.

•We find a level playing field.

Have you ever found yourself in a situation where someone has had an advantage over you because of who they knew or who knew them? Maybe you were up for a promotion at your work and all of a sudden, the boss' nephew got the job because he was, well, the boss' nephew. Or maybe you were looked over for an amazing opportunity because you were a female and they wanted a male. Life isn't always fair, is it? If we were honest, life is often more unfair than fair. I know of a family whose very young son was diagnosed with cancer. Their family was torn to pieces by the diagnosis and devastated by the treatments in which he had to endure. So many people were praying for him. Then, the young mother was also diagnosed with cancer. She is now undergoing treatment and fighting this terrible disease along with her precious son. I had this moment of deep despair at just how unfair this world really is.

Have you ever heard of the idiom "To level the playing field"? It speaks of a situation that is fair and no one has an advantage over other people. Sounds wonderful doesn't it? Can you imagine a world that is actually fair? Where no one has an advantage over anyone else? We would ALL have the SAME opportunities no matter race, gender, economic status, or social class. Sounds too good to be true, doesn't it? Well, it's not. When we compare ourselves to Christ, we find that there is a level playing field. Not when it comes to Christ, mind you, but when it comes to everyone else. See, God does not compare me to you, or you to "her". He doesn't look at each of us and compare our abilities or disabilities in light of one another. God doesn't have favorites. Romans 2:11 says, "For God does not show favoritism." Ephesians 6:9 (NLT) says, "You masters, do the same (showing goodwill) toward them, and give up threatening *and* abusive words, knowing that (He who is) both their true Master and yours is in heaven, and that there is no partiality with Him (regardless of one's earthly status)."

What does a level playing ground and no favorites mean for us? Billy Graham said, "The ground is level at the foot of the cross." No one person is better than anyone

> He sees our abilities and our gifts but doesn't see them in COMPARISON to one another.

else. There is no status to be cherished, or position to be coveted, or ability to be envied. Equal. Equally loved. Equally sacrificed for. God has the ability to love us all equally and beautifully. He doesn't hold one of us above the other. He doesn't love a preacher more than a housewife. He doesn't value a missionary more than a mechanic. He sees our abilities and our gifts but doesn't see them in COMPARISON to one another. In reality, we are all in need of Him. We ALL need His love, His forgiveness, and His grace. I found this old hymn and I think it is beautifully stated.

"The Ground is Level at the Foot of the Cross"

I stood before the cross...and a king stood by me
And on the other side...a vagabond
And there as we prayed....and poured our hearts out to
Jesus
He bent to hear everyone

The ground is level...at the foot of the cross
No man stands higher than I

I can call on Jesus' name...and a king can do the same
The ground is level at the foot of the cross!

No matter who you are...whether rich or a beggar
The call is sent to whosoever will
Just kneel at the cross...and tell the Lord that you need
Him
Your thirsty soul He will fill

No pow'r can take away, all the joy I found in Jesus,
Although the world will try my faith to shake.
God's Word is still the same, and it will stand throughout
the ages,
Your ev'ry step He'll help you take.

It's level…every piece of dirt at the foot of the cross is level. There are no dips, no holes, and no slopes. God is not comparing His children to each other, wishing one would be like the other. He isn't asking the banker to be like the teacher or the construction worker to be like the preacher. He loves us all equally and perfectly which is why He offers His salvation and love to every single one of us. When we compare ourselves to The Gold Standard, we find a level playing field…and it has a cross on it.

•We find grace.

When we compare ourselves to The Gold Standard, Jesus Christ, we find grace. The kind of grace that saves us, yes, but also the kind of grace that sustains us. God's grace for eternity as well as God's grace for here and now. The grace that is offered to us covers the sin of our yesterday, our today, and our tomorrow. Compared to the perfection of Christ, we are in need of grace. Grace beyond measure, in fact. Grace may be defined as the unmerited or undeserving favor of God to those who are under condemnation. When I began researching this word, I believe I fell even more deeply in love with the Lord than ever before. Remember how you loved your husband when you married him, but then you saw him cradle your firstborn for the first time as he gazed into the baby's face and the depth of your love for your man plunged into places far deeper than before? It's like that. When I began grasping

> When we compare ourselves to The Gold Standard, we find a level playing field...and it has a cross on it.

this idea of grace and how we are afforded something that we should never be allowed to touch, relate to, commune with…it's humbling, and exhilarating, and overwhelming. The Truth of His grace through salvation and redemption cause me to lose my breath. I *know* the depth of my sin and despair. My heart is deceitful above all and there is no good thing within me. "The human heart is the most deceitful of all things, and desperately wicked. Who really knows how bad it is?" Jeremiah 17:9 (NLT) If left to myself, I would be wallowing in the mud and the mire. But because of His great grace, His unmerited favor, He has picked me up out of the pit, wiped me clean, and decided to use me for His Kingdom. Psalm 40:2, "He lifted me out of the pit of despair, out of the mud and the mire. He set my feet on solid ground and steadied me as I walked along." Beloved, do you understand the magnitude of His actions? A Holy and Righteous God, a Blameless and Spotless Lamb, a Powerful and Mighty King, desires to not only save us with His grace but *chooses* to have a relationship with us. A living, breathing, real-life relationship with you and with me. Where we walk with Him, and talk with Him, and pour out our hearts to Him. Where He speaks to us in return, guiding us into what is not just good, but what is His best. We are unworthy of it all, beloved. Unworthy of it all. Yet, He offers it to us. Arms opened wide, ready to embrace us as children. His children. Spoken for. Loved. Redeemed. Bought and paid for by a priceless sacrifice. Jesus. When I compare myself to Him, I see grace upon grace.

A Holy and Righteous God, a Blameless and Spotless Lamb, a Powerful and Mighty King, desires to not only save us with His grace but chooses to have a relationship with us.

There you have it. The Gold Standard. Christ. If you ever REALLY want to play the comparison game, then use Him as your standard. It's a game changer, isn't it? Now, I know I told you to forget everything you previously had learned about comparison at the beginning of this chapter, but now I'm asking you to remember what you forgot. I have a feeling you'll need it. We all will.

The Gold Standard

Study Guide

1. Karen describes Christ as The Gold Standard. What does she mean by that?

_____

_____

_____

_____

2. What do we find when we compare ourselves to The Gold Standard, Jesus?

* _____

* _____

* _____

* _____

3. Which one of the above spoke to you the most and why?

_____

_____

_____

_____

_____

4. Write any additional thoughts you have about this chapter.

_____

_____

_____

_____

_____

_____

Precious Father, Abba, my Creator,

Thank you for loving each woman reading this book. Thank you for creating each of them uniquely, with a purpose.

"For you created my inmost being; you knit me together in my mother's womb. I praise you because I am fearfully

and wonderfully made; your works are wonderful, I know that full well. My frame was not hidden from you when I was made in the secret place, when I was woven together in the depths of the earth. Your eyes saw my unformed body; all the days ordained for me were written in your book before one of them came to be. How precious to me are your thoughts, God! How vast is the sum of them!"
Psalm 139:13-17 NIV11

"For I know the plans I have for you," declares the Lord, "plans to prosper you and not to harm you, plans to give you hope and a future. Then you will call on me and come and pray to me, and I will listen to you. You will seek me and find me when you seek me with all your heart. I will be found by you," declares the Lord, "and will bring you back from captivity. I will gather you from all the nations and places where I have banished you," declares the Lord, "and will bring you back to the place from which I carried you into exile."
Jeremiah 29:11-14 NIV11

I ask, Father, that these women would walk in the Truth of knowing that they are loved, cherished, and treasured by you. May they know that they are redeemed, blessed, and forgiven. I pray that they would understand the magnitude and the depth of your love for them. May they grasp the abundance of your grace and mercy. Father, may you be the only comparison we desire, to strive for and to imitate you. Thank you that you give us everything we need to walk through this life, that because of Your resurrection, the Holy Spirit, You, lives in us and gives us your fruit.

"But the fruit of the Spirit is love, joy, peace, forbearance, kindness, goodness, faithfulness, gentleness and self-control. Against such things there is no law."
Galatians 5:22-23 NIV

Help them to understand that there is nothing they can do to make you love them more, to earn your love. And that there is nothing they can do to cause you to love them any less. In your eyes, these women are Holy and blameless because of You. Thank you, Father, that when you look at us, you see us as perfect, cleansed, pure. You, beautiful princess, daughter of The One True King are loved Just As You Are, because you are You, and you are His. You are His Masterpiece!

Walk in His Truth! Amen!
This prayer was written and prayed over you by my strong and surrendered friend, Kelly Barfield.

Afterword

Whew. We made it! Oh Beloved, I can't thank you
enough for walking this journey with me. I'm humbled
and overwhelmed with your desire to see this thing to the
end. So, now what? Well, now you've been handed a
sword. A BIG sword. To fight with. To heal with. Yes,
Beloved, to heal with. This sword has a double blade.
One for battling the snake and silencing the lion and one
for bringing healing to a broken spirit. "For the word of
God is alive and powerful. It is sharper than the sharpest
two-edged sword, cutting between soul and spirit,
between joint and marrow. It exposes our innermost

thoughts and desires." Hebrews 4:12. I don't know which side of the blade you need, but He does.

I have so much in my heart for you. So much hope. So much promise. So much expectation. Know that I am praying for you. I'm praying the kind of prayer over you that brings the dead to life. The kind of prayer that brings the run-a-way home. The kind of prayer that heals a life-long, gaping, wounded heart. The kind of prayer that makes the lost found and the broken whole. I'm praying the kind of prayer over you that shakes the gates of hell and rattles the cages of those imprisoned, breaking them free. The kind of prayer that turns dry bones into armies. Beloved, I am praying the kind of prayer that turns the worrier into a warrior. Comparison has lost its grip. Satan no longer has a hold on you. He won't win. He can't. Grab your sword; stand up; prepare for battle. You are the army.

I love you. So does He.

Notes

1. Farver, Hannah. Not Good Enough. August 9, 2010. http://www.liesyoungwomenbelieve.com/not-good-enough/July 22, 2017.

2. Moore, Beth. So Long, Insecurity you've been a bad friend to us. Carol Stream: Tyndale, 2010.

3. Groeschel, Craig. Struggles. Grand Rapids: Zondervan, 2015.

4. Smith, Denise. Seeds of Purpose. West Conshohocken: Infinity, 2009.

5. Shin, Zen. https://www.goodreads.com/quotes/1135747-a-flower-does-not-think-of-competing-to-the-flower. February 5, 2018

6. http://desiringtherain.blogspot.com/2009/10/lies-satan-tells-women.html. November 15, 2017.

7. Eldredge, John. Captivating; Unveiling the mystery of a women's soul. Nashville: Thomas Nelson, 2011.

8. Warren, Rick. The Purpose Driven Life. Grand Rapids: Zondervan, 2013

9. Time. Zendaya and 8 Other Celebs Who Protested Photoshop and Won. October 18, 2015. http://time.com/3572400/zendaya-celebrities-protest-photoshop/. June 22, 2017.

10. Psychology Today. Media Exposure and the Perfect Body.

November 18, 2013.
https://www.psychologytoday.com/blog/media-spotlight/20
1311/media-exposure-and-the-perfect-body

11. Stone. W. Clement.
https://www.brainyquote.com/authors/w_clement_stone.
January 26, 2018.

12. Lombari, Vince.
https://www.brainyquote.com/quotes/vince_lombardi_3850
70. January 26, 2018.

13. Wrang, Hans. Why you should strive for excellence not
perfection. July 8, 2015.
https://www.linkedin.com/pulse/why-you-should-strive-
excellence-perfection-hans-wrang. January 26, 2018

14. Graham, Billy.
https://www.goodreads.com/quotes/7481592-the-ground-
is-level-at-the-foot-of-the-cross. February 5, 2018

15. The Ground is Level.
http://www.marmatt.com/music/songs/display.php?sn=the-
ground-is-level.txt. February 5, 2018.

About the Author

Karen Mutchler Allen is married to Lindsey Allen and they have three children: Ryleigh, Josey, and Garrison. Karen is a nationally recognized Television Show Host, a Motivational Speaker, and Author. A graduate of the University of Georgia with a degree in Education, Karen worked as an Elementary School teacher before becoming a stay-at-home mom. Inspired by her love of children and teaching, she has written a series of children's books about manners titled, *The Couth Fairy.* She is a sought after author as she travels around Georgia's elementary schools sharing her books, love for reading, and the joy of being an author. Karen has also written *The One*, an in-depth book about the joys and hardships of dating. Karen enjoys spending time with her family, the beach, reading good books, tennis, and working out. She has a passion to share the love of her Savior with others and hopes that each book she writes is a testimony to that desire. Karen and her family live in Georgia. Please visit Karenallen.weebly.com.

About the Guest Author

Michele is married to her college sweetheart, Derek Fort, and are both lifelong residents of Georgia. To commemorate their 20th wedding anniversary, the couple ran in their first half-marathon together at the "Most Magical Place on Earth". Michele is mom to three daughters: Grace, Gloria and Pearl. The first two came as gifts from the Lord the old-fashioned way and the third, a gift through international adoption. After teaching reading, writing and arithmetic in a local public school for years, Michele traded her place at the front of a classroom with a place at the kitchen table and a much smaller class. She spends her days homeschooling and carpooling the teen, the tween and the preschooler to their various extracurricular activities. She loves a good story, a good getaway, a good deal and a good nap. But mostly, she loves watching how a good God shows Himself as living and active in our everyday, ordinary lives. Though she has made written contributions to the blogosphere in the past, this is her first contribution to a book and she thanks her faith-filled friend, Karen, for believing in her and providing the opportunity.

Other books by
Karen Mutchler Allen

The One

The Couth Fairy

The Couth Fairy Returns

The Couth Fairy Goes To School

Available at Amazon.com

Made in the USA
Lexington, KY
12 March 2018